Learn German with The Red Baron and Other Stories

HypLern Interlinear Project
www.hyplern.com

Second edition: 2025, June

Author: Manfred von Richthofen, Theodor Storm, Franz Kafka, Karl Ettlinger
Translation: Kees van den End
Foreword: Camilo Andrés Bonilla Carvajal PhD

ISBN: 978-1-988830-79-7

kees@hyplern.com
www.hyplern.com

Learn German with The Red Baron and Other Stories

Interlinear German to English

Author

Manfred von Richthofen, Theodor Storm, Franz Kafka, Karl Ettlinger

Translation

Kees van den End

HypLern Interlinear Project
www.hyplern.com

The HypLern Method

Learning a foreign language should not mean leafing through page after page in a bilingual dictionary until one's fingertips begin to hurt. Quite the contrary, through everyday language use, friendly reading, and direct exposure to the language we can get well on our way towards mastery of the vocabulary and grammar needed to read native texts. In this manner, learners can be successful in the foreign language without too much study of grammar paradigms or rules. Indeed, Seneca expresses in his sixth epistle that "Longum iter est per praecepta, breve et efficax per exempla[1]."

The HypLern series constitutes an effort to provide a highly effective tool for experiential foreign language learning. Those who are genuinely interested in utilizing original literary works to learn a foreign language do not have to use conventional graded texts or adapted versions for novice readers. The former only distort the actual essence of literary works, while the latter are highly reduced in vocabulary and relevant content. This collection aims to bring the lively experience of reading stories as directly told by their very authors to foreign language learners.

Most excited adult language learners will at some point seek their teachers' guidance on the process of learning to read in the foreign language rather than seeking out external opinions. However, both teachers and learners lack a general reading technique or strategy. Oftentimes, students undertake the reading task equipped with nothing more than a bilingual dictionary, a grammar book, and lots of courage. These efforts often end in frustration as the student builds mis-constructed nonsensical sentences after many hours spent on an aimless translation drill.

Consequently, we have decided to develop this series of interlinear translations intended to afford a comprehensive edition of unabridged texts. These texts are presented as they were originally written with no changes in word choice or order. As a result, we have a translated piece conveying the true meaning under every word from the original work. Our readers receive then two books in just one volume: the original version and its translation.

The reading task is no longer a laborious exercise of patiently decoding unclear and seemingly complex paragraphs. What's more, reading becomes an enjoyable and meaningful process of cultural, philosophical and linguistic learning. Independent learners can then acquire expressions and vocabulary while understanding pragmatic and socio-cultural dimensions of the target language by reading in it rather than reading about it.

Our proposal, however, does not claim to be a novelty. Interlinear translation is as old as the Spanish tongue, e.g. "glosses of [Saint] Emilianus", interlinear bibles in Old German, and of course James Hamilton's work in the 1800s. About the latter, we remind the readers, that as a revolutionary freethinker he promoted the publication of Greco-Roman classic works and further pieces in diverse languages. His effort, such as ours, sought to lighten the exhausting task of looking words up in large glossaries as an educational practice: "if there is any thing which fills reflecting men with melancholy and regret, it is the waste of mortal time, parental money, and puerile happiness, in the present method of pursuing Latin and Greek[2]".

Additionally, another influential figure in the same line of thought as Hamilton was John Locke. Locke was also the philosopher and translator of the Fabulae AEsopi in an interlinear plan. In 1600, he was already suggesting that interlinear texts, everyday communication, and use of the target language could be the most appropriate ways to achieve language learning:

> ...the true and genuine Way, and that which I would propose, not only as the easiest and best, wherein a Child might, without pains or Chiding, get a Language which others are wont to be whipt for at School six or seven Years together...[3]

---

1 "The journey is long through precepts, but brief and effective through examples". Seneca, Lucius Annaeus. (1961) Ad Lucilium Epistulae Morales, vol. I. London: W. Heinemann.

2 In: Hamilton, James (1829?) History, principles, practice and results of the Hamiltonian system, with answers to the Edinburgh and Westminster reviews; A lecture delivered at Liverpool; and instructions for the use of the books published on the system. Londres: W. Aylott and Co., 8, Pater Noster Row. p. 29.

3 In: Locke, John. (1693) Some thoughts concerning education. Londres: A. and J. Churchill. pp. 196-7.

Who can benefit from this edition?

We identify three kinds of readers, namely, those who take this work as a search tool, those who want to learn a language by reading authentic materials, and those attempting to read writers in their original language. The HypLern collection constitutes a very effective instrument for all of them.

1. For the first target audience, this edition represents a search tool to connect their mother tongue with that of the writer's. Therefore, they have the opportunity to read over an original literary work in an enriching and certain manner.
2. For the second group, reading every word or idiomatic expression in its actual context of use will yield a strong association between the form, the collocation, and the context. This will have a direct impact on long term learning of passive vocabulary, gradually building genuine reading ability in the original language. This book is an ideal companion not only to independent learners but also to those who take lessons with a teacher. At the same time, the continuous feeling of achievement produced during the process of reading original authors both stimulates and empowers the learner to study[1].
3. Finally, the third kind of reader will notice the same benefits as the previous ones. The proximity of a word and its translation in our interlinear texts is a step further from other collections, such as the Loeb Classical Library. Although their works might be considered the most famous in this genre, the presentation of texts on opposite pages hinders the immediate link between words and their semantic equivalence in our native tongue (or one we have a strong mastery of).

---

1 Some further ways of using the present work include:

1. As you progress through the stories, focus less on the lower line (the English translation). Instead, try to read through the upper line, staying in the foreign language as long as possible.
2. Even if you find glosses or explanatory footnotes about the mechanics of the language, you should make your own hypotheses on word formation and syntactical functions in a sentence. Feel confident about inferring your own language rules and test them progressively. You can also take notes concerning those idiomatic expressions or special language usage that calls your attention for later study.
3. As soon as you finish each text, check the reading in the original version (with no interlinear or parallel translation). This will fulfil the main goal of this

collection: bridging the gap between readers and original literary works, training them to read directly and independently.

Why interlinear?

Conventionally speaking, tiresome reading in tricky and exhausting circumstances has been the common definition of learning by texts. This collection offers a friendly reading format where the language is not a stumbling block anymore. Contrastively, our collection presents a language as a vehicle through which readers can attain and understand their authors' written ideas.

While learning to read, most people are urged to use the dictionary and distinguish words from multiple entries. We help readers skip this step by providing the proper translation based on the surrounding context. In so doing, readers have the chance to invest energy and time in understanding the text and learning vocabulary; they read quickly and easily like a skilled horseman cantering through a book.

Thereby we stress the fact that our proposal is not new at all. Others have tried the same before, coming up with evident and substantial outcomes. Certainly, we are not pioneers in designing interlinear texts. Nonetheless, we are nowadays the only, and doubtless, the best, in providing you with interlinear foreign language texts.

Handling instructions

Using this book is very easy. Each text should be read at least three times in order to explore the whole potential of the method. The first phase is devoted to comparing words in the foreign language to those in the mother tongue. This is to say, the upper line is contrasted to the lower line as the following example shows:

'Was	war	das?'	sagte	er	und	hielt	die	Schaukel	an.
What	was	that	said	he	and	held	the	swing	on
								stopped the swing	

The second phase of reading focuses on capturing the meaning and sense of the original text. As readers gain practice with the method, they should be able to focus on the target language without getting distracted by the translation. New users of the method, however, may find it helpful to cover the translated lines with a piece of paper as illustrated in the image below. Subsequently, they try to understand the meaning of every word, phrase, and entire sentences in the target language itself, drawing on the translation only when necessary. In this phase, the reader should resist the temptation to look at the translation for every word. In doing so, they will find that they are able to understand a good portion of the text by reading directly in the target language, without the crutch of the translation. This is the skill we are looking to train: the ability to read and understand native materials and enjoy them as native speakers do, that being, directly in the original language.

'Was war das?' sagte er und hielt die Schaukel an.
What was that

In the final phase, readers will be able to understand the meaning of the text when reading it without additional help. There may be some less common words and phrases which have not cemented themselves yet in the reader's brain, but the majority of the story should not pose any problems. If desired, the reader can use an SRS or some other memorization method to learning these straggling words.

'Was war das?' sagte er und hielt die Schaukel an.

Above all, readers will not have to look every word up in a dictionary to read a text in the foreign language. This otherwise wasted time will be spent concentrating on their principal interest. These new readers will tackle authentic texts while learning their vocabulary and expressions to use in further communicative (written or oral) situations. This book is just one work from an overall series with the same purpose. It really helps those who are afraid of having "poor vocabulary" to feel confident about reading directly in the language. To all of them and to all of you, welcome to the amazing experience of living a foreign language!

Additional tools

Check out shop.hyplern.com or contact us at info@hyplern.com for free mp3s (if available) and free empty (untranslated) versions of the eBooks that we have on offer.

For some of the older eBooks and paperbacks we have Windows, iOS and Android apps available that, next to the interlinear format, allow for a pop-up format, where hovering over a word or clicking on it gives you its meaning. The apps also have any mp3s, if available, and integrated vocabulary practice.

Visit the site hyplern.com for the same functionality online. This is where we will be working non-stop to make all our material available in multiple formats, including audio where available, and vocabulary practice.

Table of Contents

Das erste Mal

Das erste Mal in der Luft! - Manfred Freiherr von
The first time in the air

Richthofen

Morgens früh um sieben Uhr sollte ich zum
Morning's early at seven hour should I for the
(In the morning) (o'clock)

erstenmal mitfliegen! Ich war in einer etwas
first time along fly I was in a somewhat

begreiflichen Aufregung, konnte mir sogar
understandable (state of) excitement (I) could myself even

nichts darunter vorstellen. Jeder, den ich fragte,
not there-under present Each one that I asked
(about it) (imagine)

schnurrte mir etwas anderes vor. Abends
hummed me something other -before- Evening's
(blabbed) (In the evening)

ging ich zeitiger schlafen als sonst, um am
went I more timely sleep as otherwise for at the
(earlier)

nächsten Morgen für den großen Moment frisch
next morning for the great moment fresh
(rested)

zu sein. Wir fuhren 'rüber auf den Flugplatz, ich
to be We drove there over on the airport I

setzte mich zum erstenmal in ein Flugzeug. Der
set myself for the first time in an airplane The

Propellerwind störte mich ganz ungeheuer. Eine
propellor wind bothered me quite enormously An

Verständigung mit dem Führer war mir nicht
understanding with the driver was myself not
(communication)

möglich. Alles flog mir weg. Nahm ich ein
possible Everything flew me away Took I a
If I took

Stück Papier heraus, verschwand es. Mein
piece (of) paper out disappeared it My

Sturzhelm verrutschte sich, der Schal löste sich,
crash helmet slipped itself the scarf loosened itself

die Jacke war nicht fest genug zugeknöpft, kurz
the jacket was not fast enough to-buttoned short
(tight) (buttoned up)

und gut, es war kläglich. Ich war noch gar nicht
and good it was miserable I was still at all not

darauf gefaßt, schon loszusausen, da gab bereits
there-on taken already loose to swoosh then gave already
(prepared)

der Pilot Vollgas, und die Maschine fing an zu
the pilot full gas and the machine caught on to
started

rollen. Immer schneller, immer schneller. Ich
roll Always faster always faster I

hielt mich krampfhaft fest. Mit einem Male
held (on) myself spasmodically -fast- With one time
All of a sudden

hörte die Erschütterung auf, und die Maschine war
heard the vibration up and the machine was
stopped the vibration

in der Luft. Der Erdboden sauste unter mir weg.
in the air The earth-floor zoomed under me away
(ground)

Man hatte mir gesagt, wo ich hinfliegen sollte,
People had me said where I to-fly should
told me should fly to

d. h. also, wo ich meinen Führer
that means also where I my pilot
{das} {heißt}

hinzudirigieren hatte. Wir flogen erst ein Stück
to-direct had We flew first a piece (stretch)

geradeaus, dann machte mein Führer kehrt,
straight out then made my pilot turn

nochmal kehrt, rechtsum, mal linksum, und ich
again turn right around once left around and I

hatte über meinem eigenen Flughafen die
had over my own airport the (my)

Orientierung verloren. Keine Ahnung mehr, wo
orientation lost No idea (any)more where

ich mich befand! Ich fing so sachte an, mir mal
I myself found I caught so softly on myself once
started slowly

die Gegend unter mir anzusehen. Die Menschen
the area under me to look at The people

winzig klein, die Häuser wie aus einem
tiny small the hauses as from a

Kinderbaukasten, alles so niedlich und zierlich.
child's construction kit everything so cute and fine

Im Hintergrund lag Köln. Der Kölner Dom ein
In the background lay Cologne The Cologne Dom a

Spielzeug. Es war doch ein erhabenes Gefühl, über
toy It was indeed a sublime feeling over

allem zu schweben. Wer konnte mir jetzt
everything to float Who could me now

was anhaben? Keiner! Daß ich nicht mehr
something do harm None That I not (any)more

wußte, wo ich war, war mir ganz Wurscht,
knew where I was was to me totally sausage
(not important)

und ich war ganz traurig, als mein Pilot meinte,
and I was all sad when my Pilot thought

jetzt müßten wir landen.
now must we land

Am liebsten wäre ich gleich wieder geflogen.
At the dearest were I immediately again flown
Preferably (had)

Daß ich irgend welche Beschwerden, wie etwa
That I any -which- complaints as for instance

bei einer Luftschaukel, gehabt hätte, daran ist
at an air swing had had there-on is
(air pocket) (of that)

nicht zu denken. Die berühmten
not to think. The famous

Amerikanischen Schaukeln sind mir, nebenbei
American swings are to me next by
rocking chairs (by the way)

gesagt, widerlich. Man fühlt sich unsicher darin,
said nauseating One feels himself unsure therein

aber im Flugzeug hat man das unbedingte Gefühl
but in the airplane had one the absolute feeling

der Sicherheit. Man sitzt ganz ruhig auf seinem
of the security One sits totally calm on ones

Sessel. Daß einem schwindlig wird, ist ganz
seat That one dizzy becomes is totally

ausgeschlossen. Es gibt keinen Menschen, dem
out-closed It gives no people who
(impossible) There are

im Flugzeug je schwindlig geworden wäre. Aber
in the airplane ever dizzy become were But
(in an) have become

es ist ein verdammter Nervenkitzel, so durch die
it is a damned nerve tickle so through the
(thrill)

Luft zu sausen, besonders nachher, als es wieder
air to zoom especially after as it again

'runterging, das Flugzeug nach vorn kippte, der
down went the airplane to the front tilted the

Motor aufhörte zu laufen und mit einemmal eine
engine stopped to run and with one time an
all of a sudden

ungeheure Ruhe eintrat. Ich hielt mich wieder
enormous rest in-stepped I held myself again
(silence) (entered)

krampfhaft fest und dachte natürlich: "Jetzt
cramped fast and thought of course Now
(on)

stürzt du." Aber es ging alles so
crash you But it went everything so
you will crash everything went

selbstverständlich und natürlich vor sich, auch
self-understandably and naturally before itself also
(self-evidently) (by)

das Landen, wie man wieder die Erde berührte,
the landing as one again the ground touched
(you)

und alles war so einfach, daß einem das
and everything was so simple that one the

Gefühl der Angst absolut fehlte. Ich war
feeling of the fear absolutely lacked. I was

begeistert und hätte den ganzen Tag im Flugzeug
enthusiastic and had the whole day in the airplane

sitzen können. Ich zählte die Stunden bis zum
sit could. I counted the hours until -to the-

nächsten Start.
next start.

Beobachtungsflieger

Beobachtungsflieger in Rußland
Observation flyer in Russia
(Reconnaissance pilot)

Am 10. Juni 1915 kam ich nach Großenhain, um
At the 10 June 1915 came I to Grosenhain to
(On)

von dort aus an die Front abgeschickt zu werden.
from there out to the front sent off to become

Natürlich wollte ich recht schnell 'raus, denn ich
Of course wanted I really fast there out since I

hatte Angst, ich könnte zu dem Weltkrieg zu spät
had fear I could to the world war too late

kommen. Flugzeugführer-Werden hätte drei Monate
come Airplane-driver-become had three months
(arrive) (To became a pilot)

in Anspruch genommen. Bis dahin konnten wir
in claim taken Until there to could we
claimed By then

schon längst Frieden haben; also kam es nicht in
already long peace have also came it not in

Frage. Als Beobachter mochte ich mich vielleicht
question As surveyor might I myself maybe

in meiner Eigenschaft als Kavallerist ganz gut
in my capacity as cavalryman very good

eignen; denn nach vierzehn Tagen schickte man
suit since after fourteen days sent they

mich bereits 'raus, zu meiner größten Freude an
me already out to my great joy to

die einzige Stelle, wo wir noch Bewegungskrieg
the only place where we still movement war

hatten, nämlich nach Rußland.
had namely to Russia

Mackensen ging gerade seinen Siegeszug. Er
Mackensen went just (on) his triumphal march He
{German general}

war bei Gorlice durchgebrochen, und ich kam
was at Gorlice broken through and I came
(had)

dazu, wie wir Rawa Ruska nahmen. Ein Tag im
there by as we Rawa Ruska took A day in the
former Polish city

Armee-Flugpark, dann kam ich zu der famosen Abt.
army flight park   then came I to the   famous   dep.

69,   wo   ich   mir   als Anfänger kolossal   dämlich
69   where   I   myself   as   beginner   enormously   stupid

vorkam.   Mein   Führer   war   eine   "Kanone"   --
appeared   My   leader   was   a   canon

Oberleutnant Zeumer --, jetzt auch schon krumm
over-lieutenant   Zeumer   now   also   already   bent

und   lahm.   Von   den   übrigen   bin   ich   heute   der
and   lame   From   the   others   am   I   today   the

einzige,   der   noch   lebt.
only (one)   that   still   lives

Jetzt kommt eigentlich meine   schönste   Zeit. Sie
Now   comes   actually   my   most beautiful   time   They

hatte   mit   dem   Kavalleristischen   recht   große
had   with   the   cavalry   truly   great

Ähnlichkeit.   Jeden   Tag,   vor-   und   nachmittags,
similarity   Each   day   before   and   afternoon

konnte ich meine Aufklärung fliegen. Ich habe
could I my reconnaissance fly I have

manche schöne Meldung nach Hause gebracht.
many beautiful notice to house brought
home

Juni, Juli, August 1915 blieb ich bei der
June July August 1915 remained I with the

Fliegerabteilung, die den ganzen Vormarsch
aviation department which the whole advance

Mackensens von Gorlice nach Brest-Litowsk
of Mackensen from Gorlice to Brest-Litowsk

mitmachte. Ich war als ganz junger Beobachter
participated I was as very young observer
(had)

dort hingekommen und hatte
there to-come and had
arrived there

von Tuten und Blasen keine Ahnung.
from tooting and blowing no notion
no idea about anything

Als Kavallerist war ja meine Beschäftigung
As cavalryman was indeed my occupation

Aufklären, so schlug der jetzige Dienst in mein
reconnaissance so hit the current service in my
(landed)

Fach, und ich hatte großen Spaß an den riesigen
subject and I had great joy at the huge

Aufklärungsflügen, die wir fast täglich
reconnaissance flights that we almost daily

unternahmen.
undertook

Für den Beobachter ist es wichtig, einen
For the observer is it important a

gesinnungstüchtigen Führer zu finden. Da hieß
staunch driver to find Then was called

es eines schönen Tages: "Graf Holck ist auf dem
it one beautiful day Count Holck is on the

Anmarsch zu uns." Sofort kam mir der Gedanke:
march to us Immediately came me the thought

"Das ist der Mann, den du brauchst."
That is the man who you need

Holck erschien nicht, wie man wohl glauben
Holck appeared not as man well believe

könnte, im 60-P.S.-Mercedes oder im
could in the 60 HP Mercedes or in the

Schlafwagen erster Klasse, sondern zu Fuß. Er war
sleeping coach first class but on foot He was

nach tagelanger Bahnfahrt endlich in die Gegend
after days long train riding finally in the area

von Jaroslau gekommen. Dort stieg er aus, denn
of Jaroslau come (arrived). There mounted he out / got he off the train since

es war wieder mal ein unendlicher Aufenthalt.
it was again just an unending delay

Seinem Burschen sagte er, er möchte mit dem
His boy told he he may with the

Gepäck nachreisen, er würde vorausgehen. Er
bagage travel after (him) he would go ahead He

zieht los, und nach einer Stunde Fußmarsch guckt
pulls loose / sets off and after an hour's march on foot peers

er sich um, aber kein Zug folgt ihm. So lief
he himself around but no train follows him So walked

und lief er, ohne von seinem Zuge überholt zu
and walked he without from his train overtaken to

werden, bis er schließlich nach fünfzig Kilometern
become until he finally after fifty kilometers

in Rawa Ruska, seinem Ziel, ankam und
in Rawa Ruska his target arrived and

vierundzwanzig Stunden später der Bursche mit
twentyfour hours later the boy with

dem Gepäck erschien. Das war dem Sportsmann
the bagage appeared That was the sportsman

aber weiter keine ungewohnte Arbeit. Sein
however further no unusual work His
(unfamiliar)

Körper war derart trainiert, daß ihm fünfzig
body was in such a way trained that him fifty

Kilometer Fußmarsch nichts weiter ausmachten.
kilometers march on foot nothing further mattered

Graf Holck war nicht bloß ein Sportsmann auf
Count Holck was not just a sportsman on

dem grünen Rasen, der Flugsport machte ihm
the green turn the aviation sport made him

allem Anschein nach nicht weniger Vergnügen. Er
all appearance to not less pleasure He
to all appearance

war ein Führer von seltener Befähigung, und
was a pilot of rare qualification and

besonders eben, was ja noch eine große
especially precisely what indeed even a bigger
more exactly

Hauptsache ist, er war grob Klasse über dem
main thing is he was (a) rough class over the
(relevance)

Feind.
enemy

Manch schönen Aufklärungsflug flogen wir, wer
Many (a) beautiful reconnaissance flight flew we who

weiß wie weit, Richtung Rußland. Nie hatte
knows how far (in the) direction (of) Russia Never had

17

ich bei dem noch so jungen Piloten das Gefühl
I with the still so young pilot the feeling (a)

der Unsicherheit, vielmehr gab er mir im
of insecurity much more gave he me in the

kritischen Moment einen Halt. Wenn ich mich
critical moment a support When I -myself-

umsah und in sein entschlossenes Gesicht
looked back and in his determined face

blickte, hatte ich wieder nochmal so viel Mut
looked had I again again so much courage

wie vorher.
as before

Mein letzter Flug mit ihm zusammen sollte beinahe
My last flight with him together should almost

schief gehen. Wir hatten eigentlich gar keinen
crooked go We had actually at all no
go wrong

bestimmten Auftrag zu fliegen. Das ist ja aber
certain mission to fly That is indeed however

gerade das Schöne, daß man sich vollständig
just the most beautiful that one oneself fully

als freier Mensch fühlt und vollkommen sein
as free human feels and wholly ones

eigener Herr ist, wenn man mal in der Luft ist.
own master is when one once in the air is
once one is in the air

Wir hatten einen Flughafenwechsel vorwärts und
We had an airport change ahead and

wußten nicht genau, welche Wiese nun eigentlich
knew not exactly which meadow now actually

die richtige sei. Um unsere Kiste bei der Landung
the right one be For our chest at the landing
(was) (plane)

nicht unnötig aufs Spiel zu setzen, flogen wir
not unnecessary on the game to set flew we
to risk

Richtung Brest-Litowsk. Die Russen waren in
(in the) direction (of) Brest-Litowsk The Russians were in

vollem   Rückmarsch,   alles   brannte   --   --   ein
full   back-march   everything   burned   a
       (retreat)

grausig-schönes   Bild.   Wir   wollten   feindliche
grisly-beautiful   image   We   wanted   enemy
                     (sight)

Kolonnen   feststellen   und   kamen   dabei   über   die
columns   determine   and   came   there-by   over   the

brennende   Stadt   Wiczniace.   Eine   riesige
burning   city   Wicniace   A   giant

Rauchwolke,   die   vielleicht   bis   auf   zweitausend
smoke cloud   that   maybe   until   up to   two thousand

Meter   hinaufreichte,   hinderte   uns   am
meter(s)   reached up   impeded   us   at the

Weiterfliegen,   da   wir   selbst,   um   besser   zu   sehen,
further flying   since   we   even   for   better   to   see

nur   in   fünfzehnhundert   Metern   Höhe   flogen.   Einen
only   in   fifteen hundred   meter   height   flew   One
                                 (altitude)

Augenblick   überlegte   Holck.   Ich   fragte   ihn,   was   er
moment   considered   Holck   I   asked   him   what   he

machen wollte, und riet ihm, drumherum zu
do / wanted / and / advised / him / there around / to

fliegen, was vielleicht ein Umweg von fünf Minuten
fly / what / maybe / a / detour / of / five / minutes

gewesen wäre. Aber daran dachte Holck gar
been / would be / But / there on / thought / Holck / at all

nicht. Im Gegenteil: je mehr sich die Gefahr
not / In the / contrary / ever (the) / more / itself / the / danger

erhöhte, um so reizvoller war es ihm. Also
heightened / for (the) / -so- / more thrilling / was / it / to him / Also

mitten durch! Mir machte es auch Spaß, mit
middle / through / Me / did (was) / it / also / fun / with

einem so schneidigen Kerl zusammen zu sein.
a / such / dashing / guy / together / to / be

Doch sollte uns unsere Unvorsichtigkeit bald
However / should / us / our / carelessness / soon

teuer zu stehen kommen, denn kaum war der
expensive / to / stand cost dearly / come / since / hardly / was (had) / the

Schwanz des Apparates in der Wolke
tail of the machine in the cloud

verschwunden, schon merkte ich ein Schwanken
disappeared already noticed I a swaying

im Flugzeug. Ich konnte nichts mehr sehen,
in the airplane I could not (any)more see

der Rauch biß mir in die Augen, die Luft war
the smoke bit me in the eyes the air was

bedeutend wärmer, und ich sah unter mir bloß
significantly warmer and I saw under me just

noch ein riesiges Feuermeer. Plötzlich verlor das
still a giant fire lake Suddenly lost the

Flugzeug das Gleichgewicht und stürzte, sich
airplane the balance and crashed itself

überschlagend, in die Tiefe. Ich konnte noch
overturning in the depth I could still

schnell eine Strebe erfassen, um mich festzuhalten,
fast a strut grab for myself fast to hold

sonst wäre ich 'rausgeschleudert worden. Das
otherwise were I out thrown become The

erste, was ich tat, war ein Blick in Holcks Gesicht.
first what I did was a glance in Holcks face

Schon hatte ich wieder Mut gefaßt, denn seine
Already had I again courage taken because his

Mienen waren eisern zuversichtlich. Der einzige
expressions were of iron confidence The only
expression was

Gedanke, den ich hatte, war der: es ist doch
thought that I had was this (one) it is indeed

dumm, auf so unnötige Weise den Heldentod
stupid on such (an) unnecessary manner the hero death

zu sterben.
to die

Später fragte ich Holck, was er sich eigentlich in
Later asked I Holck what he himself actually in

dem Augenblick gedacht hätte. Da meinte er,
that moment thought had Then believed he

23

daß ihm doch noch nie so eklig zumute
that (it) (to) him indeed still not so nasty at mood

gewesen sei.
been been

Wir stürzten herunter bis auf fünfhundert Meter
We crashed down until up fivehundred meter(s)
to

über die brennende Stadt. War es die
over the burning city Was it the

Geschicklichkeit meines Führers oder höhere
skill of my pilot or higher

Fügung, vielleicht auch beides, jedenfalls waren wir
ordinance maybe also both in any case were we

plötzlich aus der Rauchwolke herausgefallen, der
suddenly from the smoke cloud fallen out the

gute Albatros fing sich wieder und flog erneut
good Albatros caught itself again and flew renewed
(again)

geradeaus, als sei nichts vorgefallen.
straight ahead as were nothing happened
(had)

Wir hatten nun doch die Nase voll von unserem
We had now still the nose full of our

Flughafenwechsel und wollten schleunigst zu
airport change and wanted immediately to

unseren Linien zurückkehren. Wir waren nämlich
our lines return We were namely

noch immer weit drüben bei den Russen und
still always far over at the Russians and

zudem nur noch in fünfhundert Metern Höhe.
to-that only still in fivehundred meter height
(added to that) (altitude)

Nach etwa fünf Minuten ertönte hinter mir
After approximately five minutes resounded behind me

die Stimme Holcks: "Der Motor läßt nach."
the voice of Holck The engine leaves after
is breaking down

Ich muß hinzufügen, daß Holck von einem Motor
I must add that Holck of an engine

nicht ganz dieselbe Ahnung hatte wie von einem
not totally the same idea had as from a

"Hafervergaser", und ich selbst war vollständig
oats-carburetor   and   I   self   was   totally
(horse)

schimmerlos. Nur eines wußte ich, daß, wenn
clueless   Only   one (thing)   knew   I   that   when

der Motor nicht mehr mitmachte, wir bei den
the   engine   not   (any)more   along makes   we   by   the
(works along)

Russen landen mußten. Also kamen wir aus der
Russians   land   had to   Also   came   we   from   the

einen Gefahr in die andere.
one   danger   in   the   other

Ich überzeugte mich, daß die Russen unter uns
I   convinced   myself   that   the   Russians   under   us

noch flott marschierten, was ich aus fünfhundert
still   rapidly   marched   what   I   from   fivehundred
(which)

Metern Höhe genau sehen konnte. Im übrigen
meter   altitude   exactly   see   could   In the   rest
(For the)

brauchte ich gar nichts zu sehen, denn der Rußki
needed   I   at all   nothing   to   see   since   the   Russki

schoß mit Maschinengewehren wie verfault. Es
shot with machineguns as rotten It
        like crazy

hörte sich an, als wenn Kastanien im Feuer
heard itself on as when chestnuts in the fire
sounded

liegen.
lie

Der Motor hörte bald ganz auf zu laufen, er hatte
The engine heard soon totally up to run he had
        stopped soon totally   (it)

einen Treffer. So kamen wir immer tiefer, bis wir
a hit So came we always deeper until we
(been)   (lower)

gerade noch über einem Wald ausschwebten und
just still over a forest out-glided and

schließlich in einer verlassenen Artilleriestellung
in the end in an abandoned artillery position

landeten, die ich noch am Abend vorher als
landed which I still at the evening before as

besetzte russische Artilleriestellung gemeldet hatte.
occupied Russian artillery position reported had

Ich teilte Holck meine Vermutungen mit. Wir
I shared Holck my assumptions with We
shared my assumptions with Holck

sprangen 'raus aus der Kiste und versuchten, das
jumped outside out the chest and tried the
(plane)

nahe Waldstückchen zu erreichen, um uns dort
close forest bit to reach for us there

zur Wehr zu setzen. Ich verfügte über eine
to the defense to set I featured over a
had to my disposal

Pistole und sechs Patronen, Holck hatte nichts.
pistol and six bullets Holck had nothing

Am Waldrande angekommen, machten wir halt,
At the forest edge arrived made we (a) stop

und ich konnte mit meinem Glase erkennen, wie
and I could with my glass recognize how
(binoculars)

ein Soldat auf unser Flugzeug zulief. Zu meinem
a sodier on our airplane to-walked To my

Schreck stellte ich fest, daß er eine Mütze trug
fright set I fast that he a hat wore
concluded I

und nicht eine Pickelhaube. Das hielt ich für ein
and not a peaked helmet That held I for a
saw I as

sicheres Zeichen, daß es ein Russe sei. Als der
sure sign that it a Russian were As the

Mann näher kam, stieß Holck einen Freudenschrei
man closer came uttered Holck a shout of joy

aus, denn es war ein preußischer Gardegrenadier.
-out- since it was a Prussian guard grenadier

Unsere Elitetruppe hatte wieder einmal die Stellung
Our elite troup had again once the position

beim Morgengrauen gestürmt und war bis zu den
at the morning gray stormed and were until to the
(dawn)

feindlichen Batteriestellungen durchgebrochen.
enemy battery positions broken through
(artillery positions)

Ich erinnere mich, daß Holck bei dieser
I remember -myself- that Holck at this

Gelegenheit seinen kleinen Liebling, ein Hündchen,
occasion his little darling a little dog

verlor. Er nahm das Tierchen bei jedem Aufstieg
lost He took the little animal at each uprise
(take off)

mit, es lag ganz ruhig in seinem Pelz unten in der
along it lay all quiet in his fur under in the

Karosserie. Im Walde hatten wir es noch mit.
body In the forest had we it still along

Kurz darauf, als wir mit dem Gardegrenadier
Shortly there-on as we with the gurad grenadier
(after)

gesprochen hatten, kamen Truppen vorbeigezogen.
spoken had came troops pulled past
(marching past)

Dann kamen Stäbe von der Garde und Prinz Eitel
Then came Staffs of the Guard and Prince Eitel

Friedrich mit seinen Adjutanten und
Friedrich with his adjutants and

Ordonnanzoffizieren. Der Prinz ließ uns Pferde
ordonnance officers The Prince let us horses

geben, so daß wir beiden Kavallerieflieger mal
give so that we both cavalry flyers once
(cavalry pilots)

wieder auf richtigen "Hafermotoren" saßen.
again on true oat-engines sat

Leider ging uns beim Weiterreiten das
Unfortunately went -us- at the further riding the
(got)

Hündchen verloren. Es muß wohl mit anderen
little dog lost It must well with other

Truppen mitgelaufen sein.
troops walk along be
(have)

Spätabends kamen wir schließlich mit einem
Late in the evening came we finally with a

Panjewagen in unseren Flughafen zurück. Die
Slavic farmer's cart in our airport back The

Maschine war futsch.
maschine was bust

Im Saal

Im Saal - Theodor Storm
In the   Hall

Am   Nachmittag   war   Kindtaufe   gewesen;
At the   afternoon   was   (a) child-baptism   been
                            (had there)

nun   war   es   gegen   Abend.   Die   Eltern   des
now   was   it   towards (the) evening   The   parents   of the

Täuflings   saßen   mit   den   Gästen   im
baptized (child)   sat   with   the   guests   in the

geräumigen Saal, unter ihnen die Großmutter des
spacious   hall   under   them   the   grandmother   of the
                       (between)

Mannes;   die   andern   waren   ebenfalls   nahe
man   the   others   were   likewise   close

Verwandte, junge und alte, die Großmutter aber
relations   young   and   old   the   grandmother   however

war ein ganzes Geschlecht älter, als die ältesten
was   a   whole   generation   older   as   the   oldest

von diesen. Das Kind war nach ihr "Barbara"
of these The child was after her Barbara

getauft worden; doch hatte es auch noch einen
baptized become but had it also still a

schöneren Namen erhalten, denn Barbara allein
more beautiful name received since Barbara alone

klang doch gar zu altfränkisch für das hübsche
sounded indeed all too old-Frankish for the pretty

kleine Kind. Dennoch sollte es mit diesem Namen
little child Even then should it with this name

gerufen werden: so wollten es beide Eltern, wieviel
called become so wanted it both parents as much

auch die Freunde dagegen einzuwenden hatten.
also the friends there against in to turn had
(to object)

Die alte Großmutter aber erfuhr nichts
The old grandmother however experienced nothing
(heard)

davon, daß die Brauchbarkeit ihres langbewährten
there from that the usefulness of her long kept

Namens in Zweifel gezogen war.
name in doubt pulled was
              doubted

Der Prediger hatte nicht lange nach Verrichtung
The preacher had not long after execution

seines Amtes den Familienkreis
of his office the family circle

sich selbst überlassen; nun wurden alte, liebe,
themselves -self- over-left now became old dear
        left to themselves

oft erzählte Geschichten hervorgeholt und nicht
often told stories brought out and not

zum letzten Male wieder erzählt. Sie
for the last time again told They

kannten sich alle; die Alten hatten die
knew themselves all the old ones had the
were known to

Jungen aufwachsen, die Ältesten die Alten grau
young ones grow the oldest ones the old grey

werden sehen; von allen wurden die anmutigsten
become seen from all became the most charming

und spaßhaftesten Kindergeschichten erzählt; wo
and most joyful children's stories related where

kein andrer sie wußte, da erzählte die
no other them knew there told the

Großmutter. Von ihr allein konnte niemand
grandmother From her alone could no one

erzählen; ihre Kinderjahre lagen hinter der Geburt
tell (a story) her child years lay behind the birth

aller andern; die außer ihr selbst etwas
of all others those except her self something
(the ones that)

davon wissen konnten, hätten weit über jedes
there from know could would have far over each
older than

Menschenalter hinaus sein müssen. -- Unter
human age out be must Under

solchen Gesprächen war es abendlich
such conversations was it towards the evening

geworden. Der Saal lag gegen Westen, ein roter
become The hall lay towards the West a red

Schimmer fiel durch die Fenster noch auf die
shimmer fell through the windows still on the

Gipsrosen an den weißen, mit Stukkaturarbeit
plaster roses on the white with Stucco

gezierten Wänden; dann verschwand auch der. Aus
decorated walls then disappeared also that From

der Ferne konnte man ein dumpfes eintöniges
the distance could one a dull monotonous

Rauschen in der jetzt eingetretenen Stille
murmur in the now entered silence

vernehmen. Einige der Gäste horchten auf.
hear Some of the guests listened up

"Das ist das Meer," sagte die junge Frau.
That is the lake said the young woman

"Ja," sagte die Großmutter, "ich habe es oft
Yes said the grandmother I have it often

gehört; es ist schon lange so gewesen."
heard it is already long so been
(has)

Dann sprach wieder niemand; draußen vor den
Then spoke again no one outside in front of the

Fenstern in dem schmalen Steinhof stand eine
windows in the small stone courtyard stood a

große Linde, und man hörte, wie die Sperlinge
large linden tree and one heard how the starlings

unter den Blättern zur Ruhe gingen. Der
under the leaves to -the- rest went The

Hauswirt hatte die Hand seiner Frau gefaßt, die
house host had the hand of his wife taken who

still an seiner Seite saß, und heftete die Augen
silently to his side sat and raised the eyes

an die krause altertümliche Gipsdecke.
to the frilly ancient plaster ceiling

"Was hast du?" fragte ihn die Großmutter.
What have you asked him the grandmother

"Die Decke ist gerissen," sagte er, "die Simse sind
The ceiling is cracked said he the mantels are
(have)

auch gesunken. Der Saal wird alt, Großmutter,
also sunk The hall becomes old grandmother

wir müssen ihn umbauen."
we must him rebuild
(it)

"Der Saal ist noch nicht so alt," erwiderte sie, "ich
The hall is still not so old responded she I
(that)

weiß noch wohl, als er gebaut wurde."
know still well when he build became
(it)

"Gebaut? Was war denn früher hier?"
Build What was then before here

"Früher?" wiederholte die Großmutter; dann
Before repeated the grandmother then

verstummte sie eine Weile und saß da, wie ein
fell silent she a while and sat there as a

lebloses Bild; ihre Augen sahen rückwärts in eine
lifeless image her eyes looked backwards in a

vergangene Zeit, ihre Gedanken waren bei den
bygone time her thoughts were by the

Schatten der Dinge, deren Wesen lange dahin
shadows of the things whose being long there-to (gone)

war. Dann sagte sie: "Es ist achtzig Jahre her; dein
was Then said she It is eighty years ago your

Großvater und ich, wir haben es uns oft nachher
grandfather and I we have it us often after

erzählt, -- die Saaltür führte dazumal nicht in
related the hall door led then-to-time (in that time) not in

einen Hausraum, sondern aus dem Hause hinaus
a house space but from the house outside

in einen kleinen Ziergarten; es ist aber nicht
in a small decorative garden it is however not

mehr dieselbe Tür, die alte hatte
(any)more the same door the old (ones) had

Glasscheiben, und man sah dadurch gerade in
glass panes and one saw there-through right into

den Garten hinunter, wenn man zur Haustür
the garden down when one by the house door

hereintrat. Der Garten lag drei Stufen tiefer, die
entered — The — garden — lay — three — steps — deeper — the

Treppe war an beiden Seiten mit buntem
stairs — were — on — both — sides — with — colorful

chinesischen Geländer versehen. Zwischen zwei von
Chinese — railings — supplied — Between — two — by
— — (fitted) — — —

niedrigem Bux eingefaßten Rabatten führte ein
low — boxtree — fenced in — reductions — led — a
— — — (plantings) — —

breiter, mit weißen Muscheln ausgestreuter
wide — with — white — shells — strewn

Steig nach einer Lindenlaube, davor
steep track — to — a — linden bower — in front of that

zwischen zweien Kirschbäumen hing eine Schaukel;
between — two — cherry trees — hung — a — swing

zu beiden Seiten der Laube an der hohen
to — both — sides — of the — bower — on — the — high

Gartenmauer standen sorgfältig aufgebundene
garden wall — stood — carefully — bound up

Aprikosenbäume. -- Hier konnte man Sommers in
apricot trees / Here could one in the Summer in

der Mittagsstunde deinen Urgroßvater regelmäßig
the afternoon hour your great-grandfather regularly

auf- und abgehen sehen, die Aurikeln und
up and downgo see the Auriculas and
{flower}

holländischen Tulpen auf den Rabatten
dutch Tulips on the (green) plantings

ausputzend oder mit Bast an weiße
clearing out or with tree bark rope to white

Stäbchen bindend. Es war ein strenger, akkurater
little sticks binding It was a severe precise

Mann mit militärischer Haltung, und seine
man with military stature and his

schwarzen Augbrauen gaben ihm bei den
black eyebrows gave him with the

weißgepuderten Haaren ein vornehmes Ansehen.
white powdered hair a distinguished look

So war es einmal an einem Augustnachmittage, als
So was it once on an August afternoon as

dein Großvater die kleine Gartentreppe herabkam;
your grandfather the small garden stairs came down

aber dazumalen war er noch weit vom Großvater
but then to times was he still far from grandfather
    (then)

entfernt. -- Ich sehe es noch vor meinen alten
away   I see it still before my old

Augen, wie er mit schlankem Tritt auf deinen
eyes how he with slender steps on your

Urgroßvater zuging. Dann nahm er ein Schreiben
great-grandfather to went Then took he a writing
    (letter)

aus einer sauber gestickten Brieftasche und
from a neatly embroidered letter-bag and
    (wallet)

überreichte es mit einer anmutigen Verbeugung. Er
over-reached it with an encouraging bow He
(gave)

war ein feiner junger Mensch mit sanften,
was a fine young human with soft
    (person)

freundlichen Augen, und der schwarze Haarbeutel
friendly — eyes — and — the — black — hairpouch

stach angenehm bei den lebhaften Wangen und
stuck pleasantly with the lively cheeks and
(stood)

dem perlgrauen Tuchrocke ab. -- Als dein
the pearl grey cloth coat off — As the
(out)

Urgroßvater das Schreiben gelesen hatte, nickte
great-grandfather the writing read had nodded
(letter)

er und schüttelte deinem Großvater die Hand. Er
he and shook your grandfather the hand He

mußte ihm schon gut sein; denn er tat selten
must him already good be since he did rarely

dergleichen. Dann wurde er ins Haus gerufen,
that such Then became he in the house called
(such a thing)

und dein Großvater ging in den Garten hinab.
and your grandfather went in the garden down

In der Schaukel vor der Laube saß ein
In the swing before the bower sat an

achtjähriges Mädchen; sie hatte ein Bilderbuch auf
eight year old · girl · she · had · a · picture book · on

dem Schoß, worin sie eifrig las; die klaren
the · lap · where in · she · zealously · read · the · clear (bright)

goldnen Locken hingen ihr über das heiße
golden · locks · hung · her · over · the · hot

Gesichtchen herab, der Sonnenschein lag brennend
little face · down · the · sunshine · lay · burning

darauf.
there-on

'Wie heißt du?' fragte der junge Mann.
How · are called · you · asked · the · young · man

Sie schüttelte das Haar zurück und sagte: 'Barbara.'
She · shook · the · hair · back · and · said · Barbara

'Nimm dich in acht, Barbara; deine Locken
Take · yourself · in · guard · Barbara · your · locks
Take care of yourself

schmelzen ja in der Sonne.'
melt · indeed · in · the · sun

Die Kleine fuhr mit der Hand über das heiße
The little one carried with the hand over the hot

Haar, der junge Mann lächelte. -- Und es war ein
hair the young man smiled And it was a

sehr sanftes Lächeln. -- -- 'Es hat nicht not,'
very tender smile It has no emergency
Don't worry

sagte er; 'komm, wir wollen schaukeln.'
said he come we will swing

Sie sprang heraus: 'Wart, ich muß erst mein Buch
She jumped out Wait I must first my book

verwahren.' Dann brachte sie es in die Laube. Als
keep safe Then brought she it in the bower As

sie wiederkam, wollte er sie hineinheben. 'Nein,'
she came back wanted he her lift inside No

sagte sie, 'ich kann ganz allein.' Dann stellte sie
said she I can all alone Then set she

sich auf das Schaukelbrettchen und rief: 'Nur zu!'
herself on the little board of the swing and called Now to

-- und nun zog dein Großvater, daß ihm der
and now pulled your grandfather that him the

Haarbeutel bald rechts, bald links um die
hairpouch presently right presently left around the

Schultern tanzte; die Schaukel mit dem kleinen
shoulders danced the swing with the little

Mädchen ging im Sonnenschein auf und nieder,
girl went in the sunshine up and down

die klaren Locken wehten ihr frei von den
the bright locks blew her free from the

Schläfen. Und immer ging es ihr nicht hoch genug!
temples And always went it her not high enough

Als aber die Schaukel rauschend in die
As however the swing with a rushing sound in the

Lindenzweige flog, fuhren die Vögel zu beiden
linden branches flew carried the birds to both
(flew)

Seiten aus den Spalieren, daß die überreifen
sides from the trellises (so) that the overripe

Aprikosen auf die Erde herabrollten.
apricots   on   the   ground   down rolled

'Was war das?' sagte er und hielt die Schaukel an.
What   was   that   said   he   and   held   the   swing   on
                                                stopped the swing

Sie lachte,   wie   er so fragen könne. 'Das war
She   laughed   (about) how   he   so   ask   could   That   was
                    (that)

der   Iritsch,'   sagte sie, 'er ist sonst   gar
the   Iritsch   said   she   he   is   otherwise   at all
      {imaginary creature}   (normally)

nicht so bange.'
not   so   afraid

Er hob sie aus der Schaukel, und sie gingen zu
He   lifted   her   from   the   swing   and   they   went   to

den Spalieren;   da   lagen die dunkelgelben Früchte
the   trellises   there   lay   the   dark yellow   fruits

zwischen dem Gesträuch. 'Dein Iritsch hat dich
between   the   bushes   Your   Iritsch   had   you

traktiert!' sagte er. Sie schüttelte mit dem Kopf
maltreatet   said   he   She   shook   with   the   head
{archaic: treated}

und legte eine schöne Aprikose in seine Hand.
and put a beautiful apricot in his hand

'Dich!' sagte sie leise.
You said she quietly

Nun kam dein Urgroßvater wieder in den Garten
Now came the great-grandfather again in the garden

zurück. 'Nehm Er sich in acht,' sagte er
back Take you yourself in guard said he

lächelnd, 'Er wird sie sonst nicht wieder los.'
smiling He becomes you otherwise not again loose
Otherwise she won't let you go

Dann sprach er von Geschäftssachen, und beide
Then spoke he of business things and both

gingen ins Haus.
went inside the house

Am Abend durfte die kleine Barbara mit zu
At the evening was allowed the little Barbara along at
(In the)

Tisch sitzen; der junge freundliche Mann hatte
(the) table to sit the young friendly man had

für sie gebeten. -- So ganz, wie sie es
for her asked So complete as she it

gewünscht hatte, kam es freilich nicht; denn der
wished had came it freely not since the

Gast saß oben an ihres Vaters Seite; sie aber
guest sat up on her fathers side she however

war nur noch ein kleines Mädchen und mußte
was just still a little girl and must

ganz unten bei dem allerjüngsten Schreiber sitzen.
all down at the all youngest scribblers sit

Darum war sie auch so bald mit ihrem Essen
Therefore was she also so soon with her dinner

fertig; dann stand sie auf und schlich sich an den
done then stood she up and crept herself to the

Stuhl ihres Vaters. Der aber sprach mit dem
chair of her father That (one) however spoke with the

jungen Mann so eifrig über Konto und Diskonto,
young man so zealously about account and discount

daß   dieser   für   die   kleine   Barbara   gar   keine
that   this (one)   for   the   little   Barbara   at all   no

Augen   hatte. --   Ja,   ja,   es   ist   achtzig   Jahre   her;
eyes   had   Yes   yes   it   is   eighty   years   ago
(attention)

aber   die   alte   Großmutter   denkt   es   noch   wohl,
but   the   old   grandmother   thinks   it   still   well
                    (remembers)

wie   die   kleine   Barbara   damals   recht   sehr
how   the   little   Barbara   at that time   really   very

ungeduldig   wurde   und   auf   ihren   guten   Vater   gar
impatient   became   and   on   her   good   father   at all

nicht   zum   besten   zu   sprechen   war.   Die   Uhr
not   for the   best   to   speak   was   The   hour

schlug   zehn,   und   nun   mußte   sie   gute   Nacht   sagen.
struck   ten   and   now   must   she   good   night   say

Als   sie   zu   deinem   Großvater   kam,   fragte   er   sie:
As   she   to   your   grandfather   came   asked   he   her

'Schaukeln   wir   morgen?'   und   die   kleine   Barbara
Swing   we   tomorrow   and   the   little   Barbara

wurde   wieder   ganz   vergnügt.   --   'Er   ist   ja   ein
became   again   all   pleased   He   is   indeed   an

alter   Kindernarr, Er!'   sagte   der   Urgroßvater;   aber
old   child-joker   he   said   the   great-grandfather   but

eigentlich   war   er   selbst   recht   unvernünftig   in
actually   was   he   (him)self   really   senselss   in
(with)

sein kleines Mädchen verliebt.
his   little   girl   in love

Am   andern   Tage   gegen   Abend   reiste   dein
At the   other   day   against   (the) evening   traveled   your
(next)

Großvater   fort.
grandfather   away

Dann   gingen   acht   Jahre   hin.   Die   kleine   Barbara
Then   went   eight   years   away   The   little   Barbara

stand   oft   zur   Winterzeit   an   der   Glastür   und
stood   often   at the   winter time   at   the   glass door   and
(in the)

hauchte   die   gefrorenen   Scheiben   an;   dann   sah
breathed   the   frozen   panes   on   then   looked
breathed on the frozen panes

sie durch das Guckloch in den beschneiten Garten
she through the peephole in the snowed garden

hinab und dachte an den schönen Sommer, an die
down and thought on(of) the beautiful summer on(of) the

glänzenden Blätter und an den warmen
glistening leaves and on(of) the warm

Sonnenschein, an den Iritsch, der immer in den
sunshine on(of) the Iritsch which always in the

Spalieren nistete, und wie einmal die reifen
trellises nested and as once the ripe

Aprikosen zur Erde gerollt waren, und dann
apricots to the ground rolled were and then

dachte sie an einen Sommertag, und zuletzt immer
thought she on(of) a Summer day and at last always

nur an diesen einen Sommertag, wenn sie an den
only on(of) this one Summer day when she on(of) the

Sommer dachte. -- So gingen die Jahre hin; die
Summer thought So went the years away the

kleine Barbara war nun doppelt so alt und
little Barbara was now double so old and

eigentlich gar nicht mehr die kleine Barbara;
actually at all not (any)more the little Barbara

aber der eine Sommertag stand noch immer als
but that one Summer day stood still always as

ein heller Punkt in ihrer Erinnerung. -- Dann war
a bright point in her memory Then was

er endlich eines Tages wirklich wieder da."
he finally one day truly again there

"Wer?" fragte lächelnd der Enkel, "der
Who asked smiling the grandson the

Sommertag?"
Summer day

"Ja," sagte die Großmutter, "ja, dein Großvater. Es
Yes said the grandmother yes your grandfather He

war ein rechter Sommertag."
was a real Summer day

"Und dann?" fragte er wieder.
And then asked he again

"Dann," sagte die Großmutter, "gab es ein
Then said the grandmother gave it a
was there

Brautpaar, und die kleine Barbara wurde deine
wedding pair and the little Barbara become your

Großmutter, wie sie hier unter euch sitzt und die
grandmother as she here under you sits and the
(between)

alten Geschichten erzählt. -- So weit war's aber
old stories tells So far was it however

noch nicht. Erst gab es eine Hochzeit, und dazu
still not First gave it a high-time and there-to
(wedding)

ließ dein Urgroßvater den Saal bauen. Mit dem
let your great-grandfather the hall build With the

Garten und den Blumen war's nun wohl vorbei;
garden and the flowers was it now well over

es hatte aber nicht not, er bekam bald
it had however not emergency he got soon
that was however no problem

lebendige Blumen zur Unterhaltung in seinen
live flowers to the entertainment in his
{children}

Mittagsstunden. Als der Saal fertig war,
afternoon hours When the hall ready was

wurde die Hochzeit gehalten. Es war eine lustige
became the wedding held It was a joyful
was the wedding held

Hochzeit, und die Gäste sprachen noch lange
wedding and the guests spoke still long

nachher davon. -- Ihr, die ihr hier sitzt, und
after there-from You those you here sit and
(about it)

die ihr jetzt allenthalben dabei sein müßt, ihr
those you now all there-by be must you
(present)

waret freilich nicht dabei; aber eure Väter und
were freely not there-by but your fathers and
(of course) (present)

Großväter, eure Mütter und Großmütter, und das
grandfathers your mothers and grandmothers and that

waren auch Leute, die ein Wort mitzusprechen
were also people who a word along to speak

wußten. Es war damals freilich noch eine stille,
knew It was then of course still a quiet

bescheidene Zeit; wir wollten noch nicht alles
modest time we wanted still not everything

besser wissen, als die Majestäten und ihre
better know as the kings and their

Minister; und wer seine Nase in Politik steckte,
ministers and who his nose in politics stuck

den hießen wir einen Kannegießer, und war's
that (one) called we a pitcher pourer and was it

ein Schuster, so ließ man die Stiefeln bei seinem
a shoemaker then let one the boots at his

Nachbar machen. Die Dienstmädchen hießen
neighbor make The servant girls were called

noch alle Trine und Stine, und jeder trug den
still all Trine and Stine and everyone carried the

Rock nach seinem Stande. Jetzt tragt ihr sogar
suit after their stand Now carry you even
(rank)

Schnurrbärte, wie Junker und Kavaliere. Was wollt
moustaches   as   Junkers   and   Cavaliers   What   want

ihr denn? Wollt ihr alle mitregieren?"
you   then   Want   you   all   rule along

"Ja, Großmutter," sagte der Enkel.
Yes   grandmother   said   the   grandson

"Und der Adel und die hohen Herrschaften, die
And   the   nobility   and   the   high   lordships   who

doch   dazu   geboren   sind?   Was   soll   aus
indeed   there-to-   born   are   What   should   out (of)
        (for it)

denen werden?"
those   become

"Oh -- Adel --" sagte die junge Mutter und sah
Oh   nobility   said   the   young   mother   and   looked

mit stolzen, liebevollen Augen zu ihrem Mann
with   proud   loving   eyes   at   her   man

hinauf.
up

Der   lächelte und sagte: "Streichen, Großmutter;
That (one)   smiled   and   said   strike (out)   grandmother
                                          (remove)

oder wir werden alle Freiherren, ganz Deutschland
or   we   become   all   free-lords   all   (of) Germany

mit Mann und Maus.   Sonst   seh' ich keinen
with   man   and   mouse   Otherwise   see   I   no

Rat."
council
(solution)

Die Großmutter erwiderte nichts darauf; sie sagte
The   grandmother   answered   nothing   there-on   she   said
                                      (to that)

nur: "Auf meiner Hochzeit wurde nichts von
just   On   my   wedding   became   not   from
                                      (about)

Staatsgeschichten geredet; die Unterhaltung ging
state-stories   talked   the   conversation   went

ihren ebenen Tritt, und wir waren ebenso vergnügt
her   smooth   step   and   we   were   similarly   pleased

dabei,   als   ihr   in   euren   neumodischen
there-by   as   you   in   your   new-fashioned

Gesellschaften. Bei Tische wurden spaßhafte
companies | At (the) | table | became (were) | funny

Rätsel aufgegeben und Leberreime gemacht, beim
riddles | given up (posed) | and | liver-rhymes (limericks) | made | at the

Dessert wurde gesungen, 'Gesundheit, Herr
dessert | was | sung | Health (Bless you) | Mr

Nachbar, das Gläschen ist leer' und alle die
neighbor | the | little glass | is | empty | and | all | the

andern hübschen Lieder, die nun vergessen sind;
other | pretty | songs | that | now | forgotten | are

dein Großvater mit seiner hellen Tenorstimme war
your | grandfather | with | his | clear | tenor voice | was

immer herauszuhören. -- Die Menschen waren
always | audible above it | The | people | were

damals noch höflicher gegeneinander; das
then times | even | more gallant | to each other | the

Disputieren und Schreien galt in einer feinen
discussing | and | shouting | was seen | in | a | delicate

Gesellschaft für sehr unziemlich. -- Nun, das ist
society for very inappropriate Now that is

alles anders geworden; -- aber dein Großvater war
all different become but your grandfather was

ein sanfter, friedlicher Mann. Er ist schon lange
a gentle peaceful man He is already long

nicht mehr auf dieser Welt; er ist mir weit
not (any)more on this world he is me far

vorausgegangen; es wird wohl Zeit, daß ich
ahead gone it becomes well time that I

nachkomme."
come after

Die Großmutter schwieg einen Augenblick, und
The grandmother fell silent a moment and

es sprach niemand. Nur ihre Hände fühlte sie
it spoke no one Only her hands felt she
no one spoke

ergriffen; sie wollten sie alle noch behalten. Ein
grasped they wanted her all still keep A

friedliches Lächeln glitt über das alte liebe
peaceful smiling glided over the old dear

Gesicht; dann sah sie auf ihren Enkel und
face then looked she at her grandson and

sagte: "Hier im Saal stand auch seine Leiche; du
said Here in the hall stood also his corpse you

warst damals erst sechs Jahre alt und standest
were then only six years old and stood

am Sarg, zu weinen. Dein Vater war ein strenger,
at the coffin to cry Your father was a strict

rücksichtsloser Mann. Heule nicht, Junge, sagte er
ruthless man Cry not boy said he

und hob dich auf den Arm. Sieh her, so sieht ein
and lifted you on the arm see here so looks a

braver Mann aus, wenn er gestorben ist. Dann
good man -out- when he died is Then
(had)

wischte er sich heimlich selbst eine Träne vom
wiped he himself secretly -self- a tear from the

Gesicht. Er hatte immer eine große Verehrung für
face   He   had   always   a   great   veneration   for

deinen Großvater gehabt. Jetzt sind sie alle
your grandfather   had   Now   are   they   all

hinüber; -- und heute hab' ich hier im Saal
over there   and   today   have   I   here   in the   hall
(passed away)

meine   Urenkelin   aus   der   Taufe
my   great-granddaughter   from   the   baptism (dish)

gehoben, und ihr habt ihr den Namen eurer alten
lifted   and   you   have   her   the   name   of your   old

Großmutter gegeben. Möge der liebe Gott sie
grandmother   given   May   the   dear   God   her

ebenso glücklich und zufrieden zu meinen Tagen
similarly   happy   and   content   to   my   days
                                            (age)

kommen lassen."
come   let

Die junge Mutter fiel vor der Großmutter auf die
The   young   mother   fell   before   the   grandmother   on   the

Knie und küßte ihre feinen Hände.
knee and kissed her delicate hands

Der Enkel sagte: "Großmutter, wir wollen den
The grandson said grandmother we want the

alten Saal ganz umreißen und wieder einen
old hall totally tear down and again a

Ziergarten pflanzen; die kleine Barbara ist auch
ornamental garden plant the little Barbara is also

wieder da. Die Frauen sagen ja, sie ist dein
again there The women say yes she is your

Ebenbild; sie soll wieder in der Schaukel sitzen,
same-image she should again in the swing sit

und die Sonne soll wieder auf goldene
and the sun will again on golden

Kinderlocken scheinen; vielleicht kommt dann auch
child-locks shine maybe comes then also

eines Sommernachmittags der Großvater wieder die
one summer afternoon the grandfather again the

kleine chinesische Treppe herab, vielleicht --"
small   Chinese   stair   down   maybe

Die Großmutter lächelte: "Du bist ein Phantast,"
The   grandmother   smiled   You   are   a   dreamer

sagte sie, "dein Großvater war es auch."
said   she   your   grandfather   was   it   too

Ein Landarzt

Ein   Landarzt   - Franz Kafka
A   Country Doctor   Franz   Kafka

Ich war in großer Verlegenheit: eine dringende
I was in great embarrassment an urgent

Reise stand mir bevor; ein Schwerkranker wartete
trip stood me ahead a heavily ill waited
stood ahead of me (seriously ill person)

auf mich in einem zehn Meilen entfernten Dorfe;
on me in a ten miles distanced village
(for) in a village ten miles away

starkes Schneegestöber füllte den weiten Raum
strong snow-flurry filled the wide space

zwischen mir und ihm; einen Wagen hatte ich,
between me and him a coach had I

leicht, großräderig, ganz wie er für unsere
light large-wheeled totally as he for our
(it)

Landstraßen taugt; in den Pelz gepackt, die
country roads suits in the fur packed the

Instrumententasche in der Hand, stand ich
instruments bag · in the hand stood I

reisefertig schon auf dem Hofe; aber das Pferd
travel-ready already on the court but the horse
(in)

fehlte, das Pferd.
lacked the horse

Mein eigenes Pferd war in der letzten Nacht,
My own horse was in the last night
(had)

infolge der Überanstrengung in diesem eisigen
because of the over-straining in this icy

Winter, verendet; mein Dienstmädchen lief jetzt
winter ended my servant girl ran now
(to his end come)

im Dorf umher,
in the village around

um ein Pferd geliehen zu bekommen; aber es war
for a horse borrow to become but it was
to borrow a horse

aussichtslos, ich wußte es, und immer mehr
out-view-less I knew it and always more
(hopeless)

vom   Schnee   überhäuft,   immer   unbeweglicher
from the   snow   over-heaped   always   more unmoving
     covered over by snow

werdend, stand ich zwecklos da.
becoming   stood   I   aimlessly   there

Am   Tor   erschien   das   Mädchen,   allein,   schwenkte
At the   door   appeared   the   girl   alone   swinged

die   Laterne;   natürlich,   wer   leiht   jetzt   sein   Pferd
the   lantern   of course   who   leads   now   his   horse

her   zu   solcher   Fahrt?
here   to   such   (a) trip

Ich   durchmaß   noch   einmal   den   Hof;   ich   fand
I   through measured   still   one time   the   court   I   found
   (walked through)

keine   Möglichkeit;   zerstreut,   gequält   stieß   ich
no   possibility   distracted   tormented   bumped   I

mit   dem   Fuß   an   die   brüchige   Tür   des   schon   seit
with   the   foot   at   the   fragile   door   of the   already   since

Jahren   unbenützten   Schweinestalles.   Sie   öffnete
years   unused   pig sty   She   opened
     (It)

sich und klappte in den Angeln auf und zu.
itself and clapped in the hinges open and closed
(swung)

Wärme und Geruch wie von Pferden kam hervor.
Warmth and smell as from horses came forth

Eine trübe Stallaterne schwankte drin an einem
A cloudy stable lantern swayed there in to a

Seil. Ein Mann, zusammengekauert in dem
rope A man together crouched in the

niedrigen Verschlag, zeigte sein offenes blauäugiges
low hutch showed his open blue eyed

Gesicht.
face

"Soll ich anspannen?" fragte er, auf allen Vieren
Should I harness asked he on all four

hervorkriechend.
forth crawling

Ich wußte nichts zu sagen und beugte mich nur,
I knew nothing to say and bowed myself only

um zu sehen, was es noch in dem Stalle gab.
for to see what it still in the stable gave
(there) (was)

Das Dienstmädchen stand neben mir.
The servant girl stood next to me

"Man weiß nicht, was für Dinge man im
One knows not what for things one in the
(kind of)

eigenen Hause vorrätig hat," sagte es, und wir
own house in stock has said it and we
(she)

beide lachten.
both laughed

"Hollah, Bruder, hollah, Schwester!" rief der
Helleu brother helleu sister called the

Pferdeknecht, und zwei Pferde, mächtige
horse servant and two horses powerful
(groom)

flankenstarke Tiere schoben sich
strongly flanked animals shoved themselves

hintereinander, die Beine eng am Leib, die
behind each other the legs close to the body the

wohlgeformten Köpfe wie Kamele senkend, nur
well-formed heads as camels lowering only

durch die Kraft der Wendungen ihres Rumpfes
through the power of the turns of their rumps

aus dem Türloch, das sie restlos ausfüllten. Aber
from the door hole that they restless filled -out- But

gleich standen sie aufrecht, hochbeinig, mit
immediately stand they upright high legged with

dicht ausdampfendem Körper.
dense steaming bodies

"Hilf ihm," sagte ich, und das willige Mädchen
Help him said I and the willing girl

eilte, dem Knecht das Geschirr des Wagens zu
rushed the servant the harness of the cart to

reichen. Doch kaum war es bei ihm, umfaßt es
reach However hardly was it with him hugged it
(she) (her)

der Knecht und schlägt sein Gesicht an ihres. Es
the servant and strikes his face to hers It
(She)

schreit auf und flüchtet sich zu mir; rot
screams -up- and flees -herself- to me red

eingedrückt sind zwei Zahnreihen in des Mädchens
pressed in are two teeth rows in the girl's

Wange.
cheek

"Du Vieh," schreie ich wütend, "willst du die
You cattle shouted I furious want you the
    (beast)

Peitsche?", besinne mich aber gleich, daß es
whip recollect myself however immediately that he

ein Fremder ist; daß ich nicht weiß, woher er
a stranger is that I not know from where he

kommt, und daß er mir freiwillig aushilft, wo alle
comes and that he me voluntarily helps out where all

andern versagen.
others fail
    (refuse)

Als wisse er von meinen Gedanken, nimmt er
As knew he from my thoughts takes he

meine Drohung nicht übel, sondern wendet sich
my threat not wrong but turns himself

nur einmal, immer mit den Pferden beschäftigt,
just once always with the horses occupied

nach mir um.
to me around

"Steigt ein," sagt er dann, und tatsächlich: alles ist
Rise in says he then and indeed all is
Mount

bereit. Mit so schönem Gespann, das merke ich,
ready With such (a) beautiful harness that notice I

bin ich noch nie gefahren und ich steige fröhlich
am I yet not driven and I rise joyful
(climb)

ein.
in

"Kutschieren werde aber ich, du kennst nicht
coaching will however I (do) you know not

den Weg," sage ich.
the way said I

"Gewiß," sagt er, "ich fahre gar nicht mit, ich
Sure said he I drive at all not along I

bleibe bei Rosa."
stay with Rosa

"Nein," schreit Rosa und läuft im richtigen
No cries Rosa and runs in the true
(with)

Vorgefühl der Unabwendbarkeit ihres Schicksals
anticipation of -the- inevitability of her fate

ins Haus; ich höre die Türkette klirren, die sie
into the house I hear the door chain rattle which she

vorlegt; ich höre das Schloß einspringen; ich
puts before I hear the lock spring in I
(click)

sehe, wie sie überdies im Flur und weiterjagend
see how she moreover in the hall and further chasing

durch die Zimmer alle Lichter verlöscht, um sich
through the rooms all lights extinguishes for herself

unauffindbar zu machen.
unfindable to make

"Du fährst mit," sage ich zu dem Knecht, "oder ich
You drive along say I to the servant or I

verzichte auf die Fahrt, so dringend sie auch ist.
forgo -on- the ride so urgent she also is
(it)

Es fällt mir nicht ein, dir für die Fahrt das
It falls me not in you for the ride the

Mädchen als Kaufpreis hinzugeben."
girl as buy-price away to give

"Munter!" sagt er; klatscht in die Hände; der
Lively says he claps in the hands the
(Giddy up)

Wagen wird fortgerissen, wie Holz in die
coach becomes forth snatched as wood in the

Strömung; noch höre ich, wie die Tür meines
current still hear I how the door of my

Hauses unter dem Ansturm des Knechtes birst
house under the onslaught of the servant bursts

und splittert, dann sind mir Augen und Ohren von
and splinters then are me eyes and ears from

einem zu allen Sinnen gleichmäßig dringenden
an   to   all   senses   equally   urgent

Sausen erfüllt.
swishing   filled

Aber auch das nur einen Augenblick, denn, als
But   also   that   just   (for) one   moment   then   as

öffne sich unmittelbar vor meinem Hoftor der
opens   itself   immediately   in front of   my   court gate   the

Hof meines Kranken, bin ich schon dort; ruhig
court   of my   sick one   am   I   already   there   calm
  (patient)

stehen die Pferde; der Schneefall hat aufgehört;
stand   the   horses   the   snow fall   has   stopped

Mondlicht ringsum; die Eltern des Kranken eilen
moonlight   all around   the   parents   of the   patient   rush

aus dem Haus; seine Schwester hinter ihnen; man
from   the   house   his   sister   behind   them   one

hebt mich fast aus dem Wagen; den verwirrten
raised   me   nearly   from   the   coach   the   confused

Reden entnehme ich nichts; im Krankenzimmer
reason infer I not in the sick-room

ist die Luft kaum atembar; der vernachlässigte
is the air hardly breathable the unattended

Herdofen raucht; ich werde das Fenster aufstoßen;
stove-oven smokes I will the window open push

zuerst aber will ich den Kranken sehen.
first however want I the sick person see

Mager, ohne Fieber, nicht kalt, nicht warm, mit
Meagre without fever not cold not warm with
(Thin)

leeren Augen, ohne Hemd hebt sich der Junge
empty eyes without shirt raises himself the boy

unter dem Federbett, hängt sich an meinen Hals,
under the eierdown hangs himself on my throat
(neck)

flüstert mir ins Ohr: "Doktor, laß mich sterben."
whispers me into the ear Doctor let me die

Ich sehe mich um; niemand hat es gehört; die
I see myself around nobody had it heard the

Eltern stehen   stumm   vorgebeugt und erwarten
parents   stand   dumb   bend forward and   expect
                  (without talking)

mein   Urteil;   die   Schwester   hat   einen   Stuhl   für
my   judgment   the   sister   has   a   chair   for

meine Handtasche gebracht. Ich   öffne   die   Tasche
my   handbag   brought   I   open   the   bag

und suche unter meinen Instrumenten; der   Junge
and search under   my   instruments   the   boy

tastet immerfort aus dem Bett nach mir hin, um
gropes   still on   from the   bed   after me -away- for

mich an seine Bitte zu erinnern; ich fasse eine
me   to   his   plea   to remember   I   grab   a

Pinzette, prüfe sie   im   Kerzenlicht und lege sie
pincet   check   it   in the candle light   and   lay   it
(tweezers)

wieder hin.
again   away

"Ja," denke ich   lästernd,   "in solchen Fällen helfen
Yes   think   I   blasphemously in   such   cases   help

die Götter, schicken das fehlende Pferd, fügen der
the gods send the missing horse add the

Eile wegen noch ein zweites hinzu, spenden zum
haste because still a second there-to donate to the

Übermaß noch den Pferdeknecht..."
excess still the horse servant
(groom)

Jetzt erst fällt mir wieder Rosa ein; was tue ich,
Now only falls me again Rosa in what do I
I think about Rosa again

wie rette ich sie, wie ziehe ich sie unter diesem
how save I her how pull I her under this

Pferdeknecht hervor, zehn Meilen von ihr entfernt,
horse servant away ten miles from her distanced
(groom) (away)

unbeherrschbare Pferde vor meinem Wagen?
uncontrollable horses in front of my coach

Diese Pferde, die jetzt die Riemen irgendwie
These horses that now the belts somehow

gelockert haben; die Fenster, ich weiß nicht wie,
relaxed have the windows I know not how

von außen aufstoßen; jedes durch ein Fenster den
from outside openpush each through a window the

Kopf stecken und, unbeirrt durch den
head stick and unflustered through the
(because of)

Aufschrei der Familie, den Kranken
(surprised) scream of the family the sick one

betrachten.
watch

"Ich fahre gleich wieder zurück," denke ich, als
I drive immediately again back think I as (if)

forderten mich die Pferde zur Reise auf, aber
claim me the horses for the journey up but

ich dulde es, daß die Schwester, die mich durch
I tolerate it that the sister who me through

die Hitze betäubt glaubt, den Pelz mir abnimmt.
the heat dazed believes the fur me takes off

Ein Glas Rum wird mir bereitgestellt, der Alte
A glass rum becomes for me ready set the old one
(is)

klopft mir auf die Schulter, die Hingabe seines
pats me on the shoulder the dedication of his

Schatzes rechtfertigt diese Vertraulichkeit. Ich
treasure justifies this confidentiality I

schüttle den Kopf; in dem engen Denkkreis des
shake the head in the narrow think-circle of the
(imagination)

Alten würde mir übel; nur aus diesem Grunde
old one becomes (it) to me ill just from this ground

lehne ich es ab zu trinken.
lean I it off to drink
{ablehnen; refuse}

Die Mutter steht am Bett und lockt mich hin;
The mother stands at the bed and signals me to (her)

ich folge und lege, während ein Pferd laut zur
I follow and put while a horse loud to the

Zimmerdecke wiehert, den Kopf an die Brust des
room ceiling neighs the head to the breast of the

Jungen, der unter meinem nassen Bart erschauert.
boy who under my wet beard shivers

Es bestätigt sich, was ich weiß: der Junge ist
It confirms itself what I know the boy is

gesund, ein wenig schlecht durchblutet, von der
healthy a little bad through-blooded from the
(blood supply)

sorgenden Mutter mit Kaffee durchtränkt, aber
worrying mother with coffee imbued but

gesund und am besten mit einem Stoß aus dem
healthy and at the best with a bump from the

Bett zu treiben. Ich bin kein Weltverbesserer und
bed to chase I am no world improver and

lasse ihn liegen.
let him lie

Ich bin vom Bezirk angestellt und tue meine
I am by the district engaged and do my

Pflicht bis zum Rand, bis dorthin, wo es fast
duty until to the edge until there-to where it almost

zu viel wird. Schlecht bezahlt, bin ich doch
too much becomes Badly paid am I however

freigebig und hilfsbereit gegenüber den Armen.
generous and helpful opposite the poor

Noch für Rosa muß ich sorgen, dann mag der
Still for Rosa must I care then may the

Junge recht haben und auch ich will sterben.
boy right have and also I will die
    (justice)

Was tue ich hier in diesem endlosen Winter! Mein
What do I here in this endless Winter My

Pferd ist verendet, und da ist niemand im
horse is come to an end and there is no one in the

Dorf, der mir seines leiht. Aus dem
village who to me his borrows From the
    (theirs)

Schweinestall muß ich mein Gespann ziehen;
pig sty must I my harness pull

wären es nicht zufällig Pferde, müßte ich mit
were it not coincidentally horses must I with

Säuen fahren. So ist es.
sows ride So is it

Und ich nicke der Familie zu. Sie wissen nichts
And I nod the family to They know nothing
    And I nod to the family

davon, und wenn sie es wüßten, würden sie es
there from and when they it knew would they it
(of it)

nicht glauben. Rezepte schreiben ist leicht, aber
not believe Receipts write is easy but

im übrigen sich mit den Leuten verständigen,
in the rest oneself with the people advise
  furthermore   communicate with the people

ist schwer.
is heavy
  (difficult)

Nun, hier wäre also mein Besuch zu Ende, man
Now here would be also my visit to end one

hat mich wieder einmal unnötig bemüht,
has me again one time unnecessarily troubled

daran bin ich gewöhnt, mit Hilfe meiner
there-to am I habituated with help of my
    I am used to that

Nachtglocke martert mich der ganze Bezirk, aber
night bell tortures me the whole district but

daß ich diesmal auch noch Rosa hingeben mußte,
that I this time also even Rosa give away had to

dieses schöne Mädchen, das jahrelang, von mir
this beautiful girl that years long by me
(for years)

kaum beachtet, in meinem Hause lebte... dieses
hardly regarded in my house lived this

Opfer ist zu groß, und ich muß es mir mit
sacrifice is too great and I must it myself with

Spitzfindigkeiten aushilfsweise in meinem Kopf
sophistry to help out in my head

irgendwie zurechtlegen,
somehow lay to right
(settle)

um nicht auf diese Familie loszufahren, die mir
for not on this family to drive loose who me
to not scold this family

ja beim besten Willen Rosa nicht zurückgeben
indeed by the best will Rosa not back give

kann.
can

Als ich aber meine Handtasche schließe und
When I however my handbag close and

nach meinem Pelz winke, die Familie
after my Pelz wave the family

beisammensteht, der Vater schnuppernd über dem
together stands the father snuffling over the

Rumglas in seiner Hand, die Mutter, von mir
rum glass in his hand the mother by me

wahrscheinlich enttäuscht - ja, was erwartet
probably disappointed indeed what expect

denn das Volk? - tränenvoll in die Lippen beißend
then the people tearful in the lips biting

und die Schwester ein schwer blutiges Handtuch
and the sister a heavy bloody hand cloth

schwenkend, bin ich irgendwie bereit, unter
swinging am I somehow prepared under

Umständen zuzugeben, daß der Junge
(certain) circumstances to admit that the boy

doch vielleicht krank ist.
indeed maybe sick is

Ich gehe zu ihm, er lächelt mir entgegen, als
I go to him he smiles me towards as
he meets me with a smile

brächte ich ihm etwa die allerstärkste Suppe -
brought I him perhaps the strongest soup

ach, jetzt wiehern beide Pferde; der Lärm soll
oh now neigh both horses the noise should

wohl, höhern Orts angeordnet, die
well (from a) higher place ordered the

Untersuchung erleichtern - und nun finde ich:
research make easier and now find I

ja, der Junge ist krank.
indeed the boy is sick

In seiner rechten Seite, in der Hüftengegend hat
In his right side in the hip area has

sich eine handtellergroße Wunde aufgetan. Rosa,
itself a handpalm-large wound opened up Pink
{ref. to Rosa}

in vielen Schattierungen, dunkel in der Tiefe,
in many shades dark in the depths

hellwerdend zu den Rändern, zartkörnig, mit
brighter becoming at the edges tenderly granular with

ungleichmäßig sich aufsammelndem Blut, offen wie
irregular itself gathering up blood open as

ein Bergwerk obertags. So aus der
a mountain work during the day So from the
(mine) (That is) (a)

Entfernung.
distance

In der Nähe zeigt sich noch eine Erschwerung.
In the proximity shows itself yet an aggravation
From up close

Wer kann das ansehen ohne leise zu pfeifen?
Who can that look at without softly to whistle

Würmer, an Stärke und Länge meinem
Worms in strength and length my
(thickness)

kleinen Finger gleich, rosig aus eigenem und
small finger equal pinkish from own and
pinky finger

außerdem blutbespritzt, winden sich, im
moreover blood spattered wind themselves in the

Innern der Wunde festgehalten, mit weißen
inside of the wound held tight with white
(clung)

Köpfchen, mit vielen Beinchen ans Licht.
little heads with many little legs by the light

Armer Junge, dir ist nicht zu helfen. Ich habe
Poor boy (to) you is not to help I have

deine große Wunde aufgefunden; an dieser Blume
your great wound found to this flower

in deiner Seite gehst du zugrunde.
in your side go you to ground
will you perish

Die Familie ist glücklich, sie sieht mich in
The family is happy they see me in

Tätigkeit; die Schwester sagt's der Mutter, die
business the sister says it the mother the

Mutter dem Vater, der Vater einigen Gästen, die
mother (to) the father the father of some guests which

auf den Fußspitzen, mit ausgestreckten Armen
on the tips of the foot with stretched out arms
(tippy toes)

balancierend, durch den Mondschein der offenen
balancing through the moonlight the open

Tür hereinkommen.
door enter

"Wirst du mich retten?" flüstert schluchzend der
Will you me save whispers sobbing the

Junge, ganz geblendet durch das Leben in seiner
boy all dazzled by the life in his

Wunde.
wound

So sind die Leute in meiner Gegend. Immer das
So are the people in my environment Always the

Unmögliche vom Arzt verlangen. Den alten
impossible from the doctor desire The old

Glauben haben sie verloren; der Pfarrer sitzt zu
believes have they lost the priest sits at

Hause und zerzupft die Meßgewänder, eines nach
home and plucks apart the Mass vestments one after

dem andern; aber der Arzt soll alles leisten mit
the other but the doctor should all succeed with

seiner zarten chirurgischen Hand.
his gentle surgical hand

Nun, wie es beliebt: ich habe mich nicht
Now as it pleases I have myself not

angeboten; verbraucht ihr mich zu heiligen
offered use up you me to sacred

Zwecken, lasse ich auch das mit mir geschehen;
goals let I also that with me occur

was will ich Besseres, alter Landarzt, meines
what want I better old country doctor (of) my
would I want else

Dienstmädchens beraubt!
servant girl robbed

Und sie kommen, die Familie und die Dorfältesten,
And they come the family and the village eldest

und entkleiden mich; ein Schulchor mit dem
and   undress   me   a   school choir with   the

Lehrer an der Spitze steht   vor   dem Haus und
teacher at   the   top   stands in front of the   house and
in the front

singt eine äußerst einfache Melodie auf den Text:
sings an   extremely   simple   melody   on   the   text

"Entkleidet ihn, dann wird er heilen,
Undress   him   then   will he   heal

Und heilt er nicht, so tötet ihn!
And heals he not   then kill him

'Sist nur ein Arzt, 'sist nur ein Arzt."
It is only a   doctor it is only a   doctor

Dann bin ich entkleidet und   sehe,   die Finger
Then am   I   undressed   and   look   the finger
{sehe on; look at}

im Barte, mit geneigtem Kopf die Leute ruhig
in the beard   with inclined   head the people calmly

an.
at

Ich bin durchaus gefaßt und allen überlegen und
I   am   throughout well   and to all superior   and

bleibe es auch, trotzdem es mir nichts hilft, denn
remain it also although it me not helps then

jetzt nehmen sie mich beim Kopf und bei den
now take they me by the head and by the

Füßen und tragen mich ins Bett. Zur Mauer,
feet and carry me into the bed At the wall

an die Seite der Wunde legen sie mich.
on the side of the wound lay they me

Dann gehen alle aus der Stube; die Tür wird
Then go all from the room the door becomes (is)

zugemacht; der Gesang verstummt; Wolken treten
closed the singing falls silent Clouds step (move)

vor den Mond; warm liegt das Bettzeug um
in front of the moon warm lies the bedding around

mich; schattenhaft schwanken die Pferdeköpfe in
me shadowy sway the horse heads in

den Fensterlöchern.
the window holes

"Weißt du," höre ich, mir ins Ohr gesagt, "mein
Know you hear I me in the ear spoken my

Vertrauen zu dir ist sehr gering. Du bist ja
trust to you is very little You are indeed

auch nur irgendwo abgeschüttelt, kommst nicht auf
also just somewhere shaken off come not on
(dumped)

eigenen Füßen. Statt zu helfen, engst du mir
own feet Instead (of) to help narrow you (of) me

mein Sterbebett ein. Am liebsten kratzte ich dir
my dying bed in At the dearest scratch I you
I wish most that

die Augen aus."
the eyes out

"Richtig," sage ich, "es ist eine Schmach. Nun bin
True say I it is a shame Now ab

ich aber Arzt. Was soll ich tun? Glaube mir, es
I however doctor What should I do Believe me it

wird auch mir nicht leicht."
becomes also (for) me not easy

"Mit dieser Entschuldigung soll ich mich
With this excuse should I myself

begnügen? Ach, ich muß wohl. Immer muß ich
satisfy Oh I must indeed Always must I

mich begnügen. Mit einer schönen Wunde kam ich
myself satisfy With a beautiful wound came I

auf die Welt; das war meine ganze Ausstattung."
on the world that was my whole equipment
(only) (endowment)

"Junger Freund," sage ich, "dein Fehler ist: du hast
Young friend say I your mistake is you have

keinen Überblick. Ich, der schon in allen
no overview I who already in all

Krankenstuben, weit und breit, gewesen bin, sage
sick rooms far and wide been am say
have been

dir: deine Wunde ist so übel nicht. Im spitzen
you your wound is so bad not In the sharp

Winkel mit zwei Hieben der Hacke geschaffen.
angle with two cuts of the hoe created

Viele bieten ihre Seite an und hören kaum die
Many offer your side on and hear hardly the

Hacke im Forst, geschweige denn, daß sie
hoe in the forest be silent then (so) that they

ihnen näher kommt."
you closer come

"Ist es wirklich so oder täuschest du mich im
Is it truly so or deceive you me in the

Fieber?"
fever

"Es ist wirklich so, nimm das Ehrenwort eines
It is truly so take the word of honor of a

Amtsarztes mit hinüber."
official doctor with away-over
(to the other world)

Und er nahm's und wurde still. Aber jetzt war es
And he took it and became quiet But now was it

Zeit, an meine Rettung zu denken. Noch standen
time to my rescue to think Still stood
(of)

treu die Pferde an ihren Plätzen.
loyally the horses at their places

Kleider, Pelz und Tasche waren schnell
Clothes fur and bag were fast

zusammengerafft; mit dem Ankleiden wollte ich
together gathered with the dressing wanted I

mich nicht aufhalten; beeilten sich die Pferde
myself not uphold hurried themselves the horses
(slow down)

wie auf der Herfahrt, sprang ich ja
as on the way here jumped I indeed

gewissermaßen aus diesem Bett in meines.
(in) certain measure from this bed into mine
(so to speak)

Gehorsam zog sich ein Pferd vom Fenster
Obedient pulled itself a horse from the window

zurück; ich warf den Ballen in den Wagen;
back I threw the bale (of clothes) in the coach

der Pelz flog zu weit, nur mit einem Ärmel hielt
the fur flew too far only with one sleeve held

er sich an einem Haken fest. Gut genug.
it itself to a hook fast Good enough

Ich schwang mich aufs Pferd. Die Riemen lose
I swung myself on the horse The belts loose
(harness)

schleifend, ein Pferd kaum mit dem andern
dragging one horse hardly with the other

verbunden, der Wagen irrend hinterher, der Pelz
connected the coach wandering behind the fur

als letzter im Schnee.
as last in the snow

"Munter!" sagte ich, aber munter ging's nicht;
Lively said I but lively went it not
(Giddy up)

langsam wie alte Männer zogen wir durch die
slow as old men pulled we through the

Schneewüste; lange klang hinter uns der neue,
snow emptiness long sounded behind us the new

aber irrtümliche Gesang der Kinder:
but erroneous singing of the children

"Freuet Euch, Ihr Patienten,
Rejoice   yourself you   patient

Der Arzt ist   Euch   ins   Bett gelegt!"
The doctor is (for) yourself in the bed   laid

Niemals komme ich   so   nach Hause; meine
Never   come   I   so   to   house   my
                       (this way)   home

blühende   Praxis   ist verloren; ein Nachfolger
flourishing doctor's office is   lost   a   successor

bestiehlt mich, aber ohne Nutzen, denn er kann
steals of   me   but without use   since he can

mich nicht ersetzen; in meinem Hause wütet der
me   not   replace   in   my   house rages   the

ekle   Pferdeknecht; Rosa ist sein Opfer; ich will
disgusting   groom   Rosa is   his   victim   I   want

es nicht ausdenken.
it   not   think out

Nackt,   dem   Froste   dieses   unglückseligsten
Naked   (to) the   frost   of this   most unfortunate

Zeitalters ausgesetzt, mit irdischem Wagen,
era   exposed   with   earthly   coach

unirdischen Pferden, treibe ich mich alter Mann
unearthly   horses   drive   I   myself   (as) old   man

umher.
around

Mein Pelz hängt hinten am Wagen, ich kann ihn
My   fur   hangs   behind   on the   coach   I   can   him (it)

aber nicht erreichen, und keiner aus dem
however   not   reach   and   no one   from   the

beweglichen Gesindel der Patienten rührt den
moving   rabble   of the   patients   moves   the

Finger.
finger

Betrogen! Betrogen! Einmal dem Fehlläuten der
Betrayed   Betrayed   One time   the   false alarm   of the

Nachtglocke gefolgt, es ist niemals gutzumachen.
night bell   followed   is   it   never   good to make

Der Sanitätsdackel

————

Der Sanitätsdackel - Karl Ettlinger
The   Sanitary dachshund

Der   Held   dieser   Geschichte   ist   ein
The   hero   of this   story   is   a
           (protagonist)

        Privatier.   Keiner von den Privatiers, die in
        rentier   Not one of   the   rentier   who in
{gentleman of means}

einem Automobil elegant durch die Straßen fahren
a   car   elegant through the streets   drive

und jeden neuentdeckten unechten   Raffael
and   every   newly discovered   unreal   Raphael (painting)
                                           (false)

kaufen - o nein, ein solcher Privatier ist unser
buy   oh no   a   such   rentier   is   our

Held nicht.
hero   not

Für die Automobile   hat er gar nichts übrig   -
For   the   cars   has he at all nothing over
                              does he not want to spend anything

"mir war's genügend! Hört's mir auf mit die
to me was it enough Hear it to me up with those
Stop for my sake

Stinkdroschken, die elendigen!" - und Gemälde
stink carts the miserable things and paintings

interessierten ihn erst recht nicht. Nicht als ob er
interested him first really not Not as if he

keines besessen hätte! Gewiß besaß er eines und
no possessions had Sure possessed he one and

das hatte er sogar eigenhändig dem Maler
that had he even with his own hands from the painter

weggenommen, weil der Haderlump die Miete
away taken because the discontented rogue the rent

nicht bezahlen wollte.
not pay wanted

"Wie hieß er doch gleich, der Maler? Mit 'F'
How was called he yet just the painter With F
What was his name again

fing er an - wart mal ein Moment, wie heißt
catched he on wait once a moment how is called
started his name (now)

er denn gleich? - na, also, so ein norddeutscher
he then just now also such a North German

Kunstmaler. Ein schönes Bildl war's, lauter
art painter A beautiful little painting was it only

echte Ölfarbe, und ein nacktes Fräulein
real oil colors and a naked young lady

stellte es dar. Sauber, sage ich Ihnen, sauber! Ja,
set it there Clean say I you clean Yes
did it represent

mein Lieber, auf die nackten Weibsbilder, da
my dear on the naked woman paintings there

verstehen sich die Herren Kunstmaler 'besser'
understand themselves the gentlemen art painters better
(mastered) (artists)

als wie auf's Mietzins-Zahlen."
as how on the Landlord paying

Da es mir schon herausgerutscht ist, daß unser
Since it me already outslipped is that our

Held und Privatier Hausbesitzer ist, so will ich
hero and rentier house owner is so want I

auch gleich sagen, wo sein Haus steht. In
also immediately say where his house stands In

Schwabing. Eines von den modernen, solid
Schwabing One of those modern solidly

gebauten Häusern: wenn einer im Parterre
built houses when one in the ground floor
(on the)

niest, wackeln im vierten Stock die Kronleuchter.
sneezes wobble in the fourth floor the chandeliers

Und wenn du einen Nagel in die Wand schlägst,
And when you a nail in the wall hit

kannst du das ganze Zimmer neu streichen lassen.
can you the whole room new paint let
(again)

Aber dafür ist ein Lift vorhanden, mit dem
But therefore is an elevator before hand with which
(available)

man fahren kann, wenn er nicht gerade in
one go can when it not just in

Reparatur ist. Er ist aber immer in Reparatur.
maintenance is It is however always in maintenance

Halt, daß ich die Zentralheizung nicht vergesse!
Stop that I the central heating not forget

Das ist was Praktisches, so eine
That is something practical such a

Zentralheizung: wenn du's recht gemütlich kalt
central heating when you it truly cosily cold

haben willst, brauchst du nur den Hebel auf
have want need you only the lever on

'Warm' zu stellen.
warm to set

Dies ist also das Haus des Herrn Privatier Joseph
This is also the house of the sir rentier Joseph

(sprich Pepi) Bröselmeier, und mit Recht steht im
say Pepi Broselmeyer and with truth stands in the

Münchner Adreßbuch hinter seinem Namen das
of München address book behind his name the

stolze Wort 'Realitätenbesitzer'.
proud word real estate owner

Pepi Bröselmeier ist ein vielbeneideter Mann.
Pepi Broselmeyer is a greatly envied man

Im Schweiße seines Angesichtes hat er sich
In the sweat of his face had he himself

durchs Leben geerbt. Als er zwanzig
through the life inherited When he twenty
(come into wealth)

Jahre alt war, starb sein Vater - da hörte er auf
years old was died his father then heard he up
he stopped

zu arbeiten. Gerade als er anfangen wollte! Als er
to work Right as he start wanted When he

das sechsundzwanzigste Jahr erreicht hatte, starb
the twenty sixth year reached had died

seine Mutter - da hörte er auf, seine
his mother then heard he up his
stopped he

Mitmenschen zu grüßen. Und als er in das
fellow human to greet And when he in the

dreiunddreißigste Jahr hineinschwebte, starb seine
thirty third year floated in died his

Tante Mali - da hörte er auf zu denken.
aunt Mali   then heard he up to   think
              stopped he

Die gute Tante Mali! Achtzigtausend   Mark   hat
That good aunt Mali eighty thousand   Mark   had
                     {monetary unit}

sie ihm hinterlassen, die alte Bissgurn, die
she him left behind that old quarreler the
                                   {archaic}

Schiache! Daß mir keiner ein schlechtes Wort
angry one That to me no one a   bad   word
{archaic}

über sie sagt!
about her says

Seitdem füllte Pepi Bröselmeier seine Zeit damit
Since that filled Pepi Broselmeyer his time there-with

aus, für seine Gewichtszunahme zu sorgen und
-out- for his weight-increase to take care of and

seine Mieter zu schikanieren. Auf zweiundfünfzig
his tenants to harass On fifty two
                          (With)

Lebensjahre und einen Meter siebzig Taillenweite
life's years and one meter seventy girth

hat er's schon gebracht.
had he it already brought
         (made)

Und kein Mensch auf Gottes schönem Erdboden
And no human on God's beautiful earth surface

imponierte ihm. Von keinem weiblichen Engel hatte
impressed him From no female angel had
         (By)

er sich unterjochen lassen -- "Heiraten? Daß ich
he himself subjugate let Marry That I

nicht rutsch'!" -- höchstens zwickte er einmal
(do) not slip at most sent he once

väterlich eine Kellnerin dorthin, wo die
fatherly a waitress there-to where the

Münchner Kellnerinnen vor Erfindung der
from München waitresses before (the) invention of the

Brotkarte einen Beutel voll "Hausbrot" und
bread card a bundle full house-bread and
(food stamp)

"Semmeln hab i net" zu tragen pflegten.
buns have I not to carry used
    {Ich}{nicht}

Aber   doch   gab es   ein   Wesen,   dem   Pepi
But   however   gave it   one   being   that   Pepi
was there

Bröselmeier   bedingungslos   untertan   war,   und
Broselmeyer   without condition   be subjected to   was   and

das war "Bim", sein Dackel.
that was Bim his dachshund

"Dackel" ist eigentlich zu viel gesagt. Man nennt
dachshund is actually to much said One calls

die   Rasse   richtiger   und   wohltönender
the   race   more rightly   and   better sounding

"Promenadenmischung".   Die   Füße   waren   ja
promenade mix   The   feet   were   indeed

soweit ganz echt - wenn's nur nicht gerade ein
so far all real when it only not just a

"Dackel" hätt' sein sollen. Wäre "Bim" der Hund
dachshund had been should Were Bim the dog
(Had)

eines literarisch gebildeten Menschen gewesen, so
a literary educated human been then

hätte er vielleicht in lyrischen Stunden vor sich
had he maybe in lyrical times for him

hin gebellt:
away barked

Vom Mopserl hab' ich die Statur,
From little pugs have I the stature
(build)

Vom Fox das Kokettieren,
From fox(hound) the flirting

Vom Dackerl nur die Frechnatur
From dachshund only the cheeky attitude

Und Lust, nie zu parieren.
And lust not to obey

Ja, in Bims Stammbaum müssen schreckliche
Yes in Bims family tree must horrible

Eheirrungen vorgekommen sein! Überhaupt schon
marriage mistakes occurred be At all already

der Name Bim! Ein "echter" Dackel heißt nach
the name Bim A real dachshund is called after

uralter Münchner Tradition entweder "Waldl" oder
ancient of München tradition either little Forest or

"Maxl". Aber Bim ...!
little Max But Bim

Kam Pepi Bröselmeier zum Frühschoppen in den
Came Pepi Broselmeyer to the early-stuffing in the
{morning drink}

"Franziskaner", so sagte die Kellnerin: "Oh, das
Franziskaner then said the waitress Oh the

liebe Viech! Da geh her, goldig's Mopserl!"
sweet creature There go here cure little pug
(come)

Kam er zum Mittagessen in das "Bürgerbräu", so
Came he to the lunch in the Citizen-brew then

sagte die Kellnerin: "Und ein extraschönen
said the waitress And a extra beautiful

Knochen habe ich reserviert für Ihren Foxl!"
bone have I reserved for your little foxhound

Und abends, am Stammtisch, im "Augustiner",
And in the evening at the regular table in the Augustiner
(at his)

sagte die Kellnerin:
said the waitress

"Weil's du nur gerad wieder da bist, Schnauzerl!"
Since it you only just again there are little schnauzer
It's you again {type of dog}

Das Infamste aber war damals im
The most infamous however was there once in the
(had)

Hofgarten passiert, als er seinen Hund frei
palace garden occurred as he his dog free

herumlaufen hatte lassen - "freilich, anbinden
walk around had let freely leash
(really)

werde ich es, das arme Dackerl!" - und einen
would I it the poor dachshund and a

polizeilichen Strafbefehl über drei Mark
police punishment order over three Mark
(fine) {monetary unit}

gekriegt hatte, wegen "Freilaufenlassens eines
received had because of free-walk-letting of a
{unleashed walking}

Rattenpinschers".
rat-pinscher
{dog for rat catching}

Damals hatte er ein Eingesandt an die Zeitung
That time had he a submission to the newspaper
            (letter)

geschickt, ein Eingesandt - na, Aufsehen   hätt's
sent   a   submission   well sensation it would have

gemacht, wenn sie's veröffentlicht hätten.
made   when they it   published   had

Aber sie haben's nicht veröffentlicht. Vielleicht
But they had it not   published   Maybe

 weil's zu lang war. Vielleicht auch weil er den
because it too long was Maybe   also because he the

Hundeaufseher   darin   einen "geselchten Affen"
dog-watcher   there-in a   smoked   monkey
(dog catcher)

genannt hatte.
called had

Ha, die Redakteure! Die reinen Kunstmaler sind's!
Ha that editor The pure   artists   are it
                                                (are they)

Und einen Menschen, der solchene Eingesandts
And a human who such a submission

schreiben konnte, tyrannisierte Bim, der Dackel,
write could bullied Bim the dachshund
(was bullied by)

obwohl er kaum den zehnten Teil so viel wog
even though he hardly the tenth part so much weighed

als sein Herrle (einschließlich Hundemarke).
as his little master including dog tag

Denn was ist des Menschen Wille gegen den
Since what is the human's will against the

Willen eines Dackels?
will of a dachshund

Hundertmal schon hatte der Hausarzt zu Herrn
(A) Hundred times already had the house-doctor to Mr

Bröselmeier gesagt: "Herr Realitätenbesitzer, Sie
Broselmeyer said Mr real estate owner you

sollten sich mehr Bewegung machen! Das viele
should yourself more movement make The much
move around more

Fett ist nicht gut für Ihr Herz, Herr
fat   is   not   good for your heart   Mr

Realitätenbesitzer! Mehr zu Fuß gehen sollten Sie,
real estate owner   More by foot go   should   you

Herr Realitätenbesitzer!"
Mr   real estate owner

"Meinen Sie wirklich?" hatte Pepi gefragt. "Also
Mean   you really   had   Pepi asked   Well

dann werde ich um   und anlaufen wie ein
then shall   I   around and on-walk   as   a

Heuschrecken!"   und heimlich   hatte er   sich
hay-scare   and secretly   had   he   himself
(grasshopper)

gedacht: "Den Buckel   steigst mich   hinauf,
thought   The   humpback rises   myself up

Medizinlackel, damischer!"
medicine gawk   conman

Und   hatte sich   auf der Trambahn ein
And   had   himself on   the tramway   a

Jahresabonnement genommen.
year's subscription taken

Aber was der Hausarzt trotz eindringlicher
But what the house-doctor in spite of urget

Ermahnung und gesalzenster Rechnungen nicht
admonition and salty bills not
(steep)

erreicht hatte, das vollbrachte Bim, der Dackel,
reached had that achieved Bim the dachshund
(accomplished)

ohne ein Wort zu reden, ohne mit seinem
without a word to speak without with his

Mopsschwanzerl zu wackeln. Denn in der
little pug tail to wiggle Then in the

Münchner Trambahn ist das Mitnehmen von
from München tramway is the taking along of

Hunden verboten, und so mußte Herrle
dogs forbidden and thus must little Mr

Bröselmeier die Riesenstrecken Schwabing -
Broselmeyer the giant stretch Schwabing to

Franziskaner,   Franziskaner - Bürgerbräu,
Franziskaner (pub)   Franziskaner (pub) to Bürgerbräu (pub)

Bürgerbräu - Augustiner, Augustiner -
Bürgerbräu (pub) to Augustiner (pub) Augustiner (pub) to

Schwabing keuchend zu Fuß zurücklegen.
Schwabing coughing by foot lay back
      (panting)   (return)

Ja, er mußte jeden Weg mindestens dreimal
Yes he must each way at least three times

wandeln, denn Bim hatte die selbstherrliche
walk since Bim had the highhanded

Gewohnheit, im Zickzack zu traben. Bald
habit in the zig-zag to trot Soon

interessierte ihn weit vorne irgendeine
interested him far in front some

Hundesensation, und er sauste plötzlich davon,
dog sensation and he rushed suddenly there-from

daß sein Herr unter Atembeschwerden und völlig
that his master under heavy breathing and fully
      (owner)

zwecklosen "Bim, da gehst her!" - Rufen ihm
senseless Bim then go here Calls him
(useless) come over here

nachstürzen mußte - bald fiel es Herrn Bim
after rush must soon fell it Mr Bim

plötzlich ein, daß er eine Straßenecke zu
suddenly in that he a street corner to

beschnuppern vergessen hatte und er machte
sniff forgot had and he made

kehrt, lief dreißig Meter zurück, beschnüffelte das
turn ran thirty meters back sniffed the

Eckhaus einmal, zweimal, um dann - nun ja, ein
corner house once twice for then now yes a

Viech is immer ein Viech!
creature is always a creature

Manchmal auch überkam ihn die Philosophitis, er
Often also overcame him the philisophitis he

setzte sich mitten auf die Straße, versank in
set himself middle on the street sunk in

Nachdenken und war durch keinerlei Zureden
pondering and was through none at all talking to
by no means

zum Weitergehen zu bewegen.
to the further going to move
to be convinced to continue

Natürlich hätte Herr Bröselmeier in solchen
Of course had Mr Broselmeyer in such

Fällen von seinem Spazierstock mit dem
occurrences from his cane with the

Hirschgeweihgriff, der wie beinahe echt aussah,
deer-antler-grip which as almost real looked
(handle out of deer antler)

Gebrauch machen können, aber nein: "Und an
use make could but no And to

einem wehrlosen Tier werde ich mich vergreifen,
a defenseless animal will I mysef abuse

- ich bin doch kein Ruß!"
I am indeed no Russian

So lebten Bim als Gebieter und Herr Bröselmeier
So lived Bim as commander and Mr Broselmeyer

als folgsamer Untergebener friedlich zusammen -
as submissive subject peacefully together

bis der Weltkrieg auch diese Harmonie zweier
until the World War also this harmony of two

schöner Seelen jäh zu zerstören drohte.
beautiful souls abruptly to destroy threatened

Der Krieg. Anfangs fand ihn Pepi Bröselmeier
The war In the beginning found him Pepi Broselmeyer
(it)

ganz schön. Er hielt es für ganz in der Ordnung,
totally beautiful He held it for totally in the order
ok

daß sich andere Leute totschießen ließen,
that themselves other people dead shoot let

damit er ruhig seinen Frühschoppen weiter
there-with he calmly his early-stuffing further
(so) (morning drink)

trinken konnte. Er schaffte sogar für sein
drink could He acquired even for his
{anschaffen; to acquire}

Haus eine Fahne an und überließ es der
house a flag on and let over it (to) the

Hausmeisterin,   sie   nach   Gutdünken
house mistress   herself   to   discretion
(concierge)

herauszuhängen oder einzuziehen. Aber bald kamen
to hang out   or   to pull in   But   soon   came

die Beschwerden.
the   complaints

Mit   einem   Herrn   im   Zylinder   fing es an.
With   a   gentleman   in   cylinder hat   caught   it   on
                        (high hat)   it started

Der   kam eines Morgens um acht Uhr, wenn ein
That one came   one   morning   at   eight   hour   when   a
                                  o'clock

anständiger   Bürger   noch   im   Bett   liegt,   und
decent   citizen   still   in   bed   lies   and

klingelte.   Er   müsse   den   Herrn
rang   He   must   the   gentleman (of the house)

sprechen.
speak to

Bim   bellte,   wie   nur   der   Hund   des   "Hausherrn"
Bim   barked   as   only   the   dog   of the   lord of the house

bellen darf, und Herr Bröselmeier schlüpfte
bark may and Mr Broselmeyer shuffled

mißmutig in seinen Schlafrock, machte Toilette,
sullenly in his sleep-skirt made toilet
(dressing gown)

indem er einmal schnell mit der Hand durch die
in that he once quickly with the hand through the

Haare fuhr, schlüpfte in die Pantoffeln - "Jessas,
hair carried shuffled in the slippers Geez
(put)

wo hat das Hundsviech wieder den anderen
who had that dog-creature again the other

Pantoffel hinbracht?!" - und schlürfte in den
slipper to-brought and slurped in the
(carried away) {bummed}

Salon, wo das nackte Fräulein hing von dem
living room where the naked young lady hung from the

Maler, der wo mit "F" anfängt.
painter the one who with F started

Und was wollte der Zylindermann? Herr
And what wanted the cylinder (hat) man Mr

Bröselmeier   möchte   doch   in   den
Broselmeyer   may   indeed   in   the

Wohlfahrtsausschuß seines Bezirkes eintreten, der
charity fund   of his   district   enter   the

Herr Weckerlbacher sei auch drin und es sei
Mr   Weckerlbacher   were   also   there in   and   it   were

doch ein guter Zweck und...
indeed   a   good   cause   and

Er warf den Mann hinaus. "Geht nicht, geht
He   threw   the   man   out   Goes   not   goes
Is not possible

beim besten Willen nicht! I habe keine Zeit, ich
by the   best   will   not   I   have   no   time   I
even if I wanted

bin Privatier!"
am   rentier

Nicht als ob unser Held ein hartes Herz gehabt
Not   as   if   our   hero   a   hard   heart   had

hätte. Gewiß nicht. Nur keine Arbeit durfte man
would have   Surely   not   Only   no   work   should   one

nicht von ihm verlangen. O, er tat auch was
not from him desire Oh he did also something

für die Armen! In der Zeitung in der öffentlichen
for the poor In the newspaper in the public

Massenquittung über freiwillige Spenden, stand's
mass receipt about volunteer expenses stood it

deutlich zu lesen:
clearly to read

N. N.: 100 Mk., Gott lohne es: 250 Mk., Jeder
N N 100 Mark God reward it 250 Mark Everyone

nach seinen
after his

Kräften: 75 Mk., Joseph Bröselmeier,
strengths 75 Mark Joseph Broselmeyer

Realitätenbesitzer:
Real estate owner

5 Mk., Ungenannt: 100 Mk.
5 Mark Unnamed 100 Mark
(Anonymous)

Die zweite Unannehmlichkeit, die ihm der Krieg
The second inconvenience that him the war

bescherte, war die peinliche Erfahrung, daß
granted was the painful experience that

mehrere Mieter um Nachlaß baten. Und da zeigte
multiple tenants for discount bade And then showed
(asked)

es sich, daß Pepi doch kein Unmensch war:
it itself that Pepi indeed no inhuman was
(monster)

denen, die's nötig hatten, ermäßigte er die
the ones which it necessary had reduced he the
who needed it

Miete großmütig. "Ja, ja, is schon recht! Wann
rent magnanimous Yes yes (it) is already right When

Ihr Mann aus dem Krieg heimkommt, nachher
your man from the war home comes after

gilt aber wieder der alte Mietpreis! Nichts zu
is valid however again the old rent Nothing to

danken, Frau Huber, nichts zu danken!"
thank Mrs Huber nothing to thank

Die   dritte   Unannehmlichkeit   war   die   Wut   über
The   third   inconvenience   was   the   anger   about

den   Hindenburg.   Jawohl,   die   Wut   über   den
-the-   Hindenburg   Yes   the   anger   about   -the-

Hindenburg.   Ist   das   vielleicht   ein   Benehmen   von
Hindenburg   It is   that   maybe   a   behavior   of

diesem   Mann,   eine   so   höfliche   Ansichtskarte
this   man   a   such   polite   postcard

überhaupt   nicht   zu   beantworten?   Dem   einbeinigen
at all   not   to   answer   The   one legged

Hausierer   im   "Augustiner"   hatte   er   die   Karte
peddler   in the   Augustiner   had   he   the   card

abgekauft,   ein   Mann   war   drauf   abgemalt,   der   aus
bought of   a   man   was   there on   pictured   who   from

dem   Spundloch   eines   Bierfasses   trank   und
the   bunghole   of a   beer barrel   drank   and

darunter   stand   "Nur   kein   Wasser   nicht"   -   und   so
there under   stood   Only   no   water   nog   and   so

eine   Postkarte   ließ   der   Hindenburg   einfach
a   postcard   let   the   Hundenburg   simply

unbeantwortet!
unanswered

Pepi   Bröselmeier   gab   der   Hausmeisterin   den
Pepi   Broselmeyer   gave   the   house mistress   the
                                                 (concierge)

strengen   Befehl,   bei   keinem   der   Hindenburg-Siege
strict   order   at   none   of the   Hindenburg wins

mehr   zu   flaggen.   Das   war   seine   Rache.
(any)more   to   hang out the flag   That   was   his   revenge

Nein,   der   Kriegszustand   war   nicht   schön.   Der
No   the   state of war   was   not   beautiful   The

Krieg   wurde   immer   länger   und   die   Weißwürscht'
war   became   always   longer   and   the   white sausage

immer   kürzer.   Das   einzig   Erfreuliche   war,   daß   sie,
always   shorter   The   only   gratifying   was   that   they

ganz   im   Anfang,   den   Riedingerfranz,   den   er
all   in the   beginning   the   Riedingerfranz   who   he

schon lange nicht leiden konnte, am Stachus
already long not suffer could at the Stachus

elendig zusammengehaut hatten, weil er
miserably together chopped had because he
(beaten up)

irrtümlicherweise für einen Spion gehalten worden
accidentally for a spy held became

war.
was

Das Schlimmste aber -- doch nein, das muß ich
The worst however indeed no that must I

ausführlich erzählen.
extensively relate

"Du, Pepi, da mußt schon in dein' Beutel
You Pepi there must (you) already in your bag

langen und ein Büllett kaufen," hatte einer seiner
reach and a ticket to buy had one of his
{billet}

Stammtischkumpane gesagt und ihm gleich ein
regular table companions said and him immediately a

Drei-Mark-Büllett hingelangt. "Es ist zum Besten
three mark ticket   to-reached   It   is   to the   best
{billet}

von die Verwundeten! In die 'Vier Jahreszeiten'!
of the wounded (ones) In the four year's times
(seasons)

Mit einem extra-igen Programm! Also ruckst halt
With a extraordinary program Also pull even

raus mit deinen Taler!"
out with your talers
{money}

Was war da zu machen? Der Pepi ruckte den
What was there to make The Pepi pulled the
(do)

Taler heraus und ging am nächsten Abend in die
Talers out and went at the next evening in the
{money}

"Vier Jahreszeiten".
four seasons

Alles, was wahr ist, es war ein extra-iges
All what true is it was a extraordinary

Programm.
program

Zuerst hat ein Herr Klavier gespielt, so
First had a gentleman (upright) piano played so

schön wie ein Athlet hat er gespielt. Zum Sterben
beautiful as an athlete had he played To the dying

fad ist es dem Pepi Bröselmeier vorgekommen,
bland is it to the Pepi Broselmeyer occurred

und er hat sich gewundert, daß der Hausherr
and he had himself wondered that the house master

von den "Vier Jahreszeiten" das erlaubt hat.
of the four seasons it allowed had

Aber Prinz Ludwig Ferdinand war auch da und
But prince Ludwig Ferdinand was also there and

hat fest applaudiert. Er hatte doch ein gutes
had steadily applauded He had indeed a good

Herz, der Ludwig Ferdinand. Und da haben der
heart -the- Ludwig Ferdinand And then have the

Pepi und die anderen Leut' auch geklatscht.
Pepi and the other people also clapped

Dann ist eine Sängerin gekommen.
Then is a female singer come
    (has)

Sie hat zwar einen Kropf gehabt, aber jodeln hat
She had indeed a throat -had- but yodeling had

sie doch nicht können.
she however not been able to

Sondern er war nur zur Verzierung da, der
But he was only to the decoration there the

Kropf.
crop

Aber dann! O, das war drei Markl wert! Dann
But then Oh that was three little Marks worth Then

kam ein Herr und hat einen Vortrag gehalten
came a gentleman and had a lecture held

mit Lichtbildern. Über die Sanitätshunde.
with light images About the sanitary dogs
    (photographs)

Der Pepi hat nur gerade so gestaunt.
The Pepi had only just so marveled

Das Herz ist ihm aufgegangen. So gescheite
The heart had him gone up Such clever

Hunde! Ja, sollt man's denn für möglich halten?
dogs Yes should one it then for possible hold
(assume)

Pepi Bröselmeier geriet in Ekstase. Das ist ja
Pepi Broselmeyer got in extasy That is yes

großartig mit den Sanitätshunden! Ja, dafür
great with the sanitary dogs Yes therefore

würde er auch was stiften! Fünf Mark, zehn
would he also something donate Five Mark ten
{money}

Mark, -- ach was, Pepi, sei kein Geizkragen:
Mark Oh whatever Pepi be not (a) scrooge
{money}

zwanzig Mark, jawohl, zwanzig Markln!
twenty Mark yes twenty little Marks
{money} {money}

Der Pepi war ganz begeistert. Und er ist
-The- Pepi was totally enthusiastic And he is
(very)

gleich Mitglied vom Verein für die
immediately member from the Society for the

Sanitätshunde geworden.
Sanitary dogs become

Und wie er beim Herausgehen seinen Bim an der
And as he with the going out his Bim at the

Garderobe wieder in Empfang genommen hat, da
cloakroom again in reception took had then
received

hat er ihn noch zärtlicher angeschaut als sonst,
had he him even more tender looked at as before

und hat ihn liebevoll gepatscht und hat gesagt: "Ja,
and had him full of love smacked and had said Yes
(patted)

das Viecherln! So ein Bim is gescheiter als ich!"
that little creature Such a Bim is more clever than I

Und da hat er recht gehabt, der Herr
And then had he right had the Mr
been correct

Realitätenbesitzer.
real estate owner

Aber unterwegs, auf dem Weg zum Stammtisch,
But underway on the road to the regular table

fiel unserm Pepi ein Satz aus dem Vortrag ein,
fell our Pepi a sentence from the lecture in

ein Satz, der ihn schon in den "Vier
a sentence that him already in the four

Jahreszeiten" gegiftet hatte, und seine gute Laune
seasons riled had and his good mood

schmolz merklich zusammen. Was hatte der Herr
melted noticeably together What had the Mr
(away)

Redner gesagt? "Am besten eignen sich zum
lecturer said At the best suit themselves to the

Sanitätshund die deutschen Schäferhunde!"
sanitary dog the German shepherd-dogs
(shepherds)

War das nicht eine Beleidigung für seinen Bim?
Was that not an insult for his Bim

Glaubte der obergescheite Herr im Frack
Believed the overclever Mr in the tailcoat

vielleicht, die Dackeln sind dümmer als wie die
maybe the dachshund are dumber as like the

"langhaarigen" Hunde? War net übel! Ein so ein
longheared dogs Was just nasty One such a

gescheites Tier als wie einen Dackel gibt es
clever animal as like a dachshund gives it
is there

überhaupt keins mehr in dieser Zoologie!
at all none (any)more in this zoology

"Gelt, Bim, du bist gescheit?" frug Herr
Is valid Bim you are clever asked Mr
{Right? (interjection)}

Bröselmeier zärtlich, aber Bim gab keine Antwort,
Broselmeyer tenderly but Bim gave no answer

weil er gerade mal wieder auf das andere
because he just once again on the other

Trottoir hinübergelaufen war.
sidewalk walked over to was

Und wenn dieser Mensch im Frack behauptete,
And when this person in the tailcoat claimed

die Schäferhunde eigneten sich am besten,
the shepherd dogs suited themselves -at- the best

so   kam   das   einfach   daher,   weil   er   noch
then   came   that   simply   there-from   because   he   yet

keinen   Versuch   mit   einem   "Dackel"   gemacht   hatte!
no   try   with   a   dachshund   made   had

Und   plötzlich   durchzuckte   den   Herrn
And   suddenly   through twitched   -the-   Mr

Realitätenbesitzer   ein   genialer   Gedanke: "Der   Bim
real estate owner   a   ingenious   thought   The   Bim

muß   Sanitätshund   werden!   Ein   'Sanitätsdackel'   muß
must   sanitary dog   become   A   sanitary dachshund   must

er   werden!   Damit   daß   das   saudumme   Gerede
he   become   There with   that   the   sow-dumb   talk
(So)

von   dem   Schäferhund   einmal   ein   Ende   hat!"
of   the   shepherd -dog-   one time   an   end   has

Wenn   der   Pepi   Bröselmeier   einmal   einen   Entschluß
When   the   Pepi   Broselmeyer   one time   a   decision

gefaßt   hat,   dann   wird   er   auch   ausgeführt.   Und
taken   had   then   became   he   also   executed   And
(it)

wenn sich gleich der ganze "Augustiner" auf
when itself immediately the whole Augustiner on

den Kopf stellt.
the head sets

"... Was hatte denn das Herrle heute?" dachte
What had then the little master today thought

sich Bim einige Tage später und
himself Bim some days later and

beguckte verurteilend seinen Besitzer. "Was hat er
looked at condemning his possessor What has he
looked disapprovingly at (owner)

denn?"
then

Vor ihm stand Herr Pepi, in der einen Hand eine
Before him stood Mr Pepi in the one hand a

feldgraue Soldatenmütze, die er Gott weiß wo
fieldgrey soldier-hat which he God knows where

aufgetrieben hatte, in der anderen Hand einen
upfloated had in the other hand a

Mordsspaten, und lockte: "Komm her, Bim, komm
murder spade / and / lured / Come / here / Bim / come
(huge spade)

schön her! Spazieren geht der gute Hund! Gassi
already / here / Walking / goes / the / good / dog / Streetie

gehen, Bim!"
go / Bim

Aber der gute Hund dachte sich: "Geh nur
But / the / good / dog / thought / (by) himself / Go / just

du Gassi, ich bleibe zu Hause!", watschelte an
you(rself) / streetie / I / stay / at / home / waddled / to

seinen Freßnapf, stärkte sich und läpperte
his / foodbowl / strengthened / himself / and / lapped
(fed)

dann am Wasserteller ein paar Tropfen.
then / at the / waterbowl / a / few / drops

Kopfschüttelnd sah ihm Pepi zu. "Wo er nur
Head shaking / looked / him / Pepi / at / (From) Who / he / just
looked Pepi at him

das viele Wassersaufen her hat! Von mir hat er's
that / much / water drinking / away / had / From / me / had / he it

nicht!"
not

Bim wartete nicht ab, bis sein Herrle dieses
Bim waited not off until his little master this
    did not await

Rätsel gelöst hatte; er war aufs Bett gesprungen
solution solved had he was on the bed jumped

und bereitete sich auf ein Schlummerstündchen
and prepared himself -on- a little nap hour
  {bereitete vor}

vor. Da nahm Herr Bröselmeier sein Dackerl auf
for Then took Mr Broselmeyer his dachshund on

den Arm und trug ihn, nebst Spaten und
the arm and carried him next (to) spade and

Soldatenmütze, die Treppe hinunter.
soldier hat the stairs down

"Also dann!" dachte Bim. "Wenn er mich trägt,
Also then thought Bim When he me carries

laufe ich mit!"
walk I along

Ach, was sind Hoffnungen? Vor der Haustüre
Oh what are hopes In front of the house door

setzte Pepi den Hund auf den Boden, und nun
set Pepi the dog on the ground and now

ging es die Franz-Joseph-Straße hinunter, die
went it the Franz-Joseph-street down the

Leopold-Straße, die Ludwig-Straße entlang.
Leopold-street the Ludwig-street along

Bim stutzte zum zweiten Male. "Jetzt weiß das
Bim stopped short for the second time Now knows the

Herrle nicht mehr den Weg zum
little master not (any)more the road to the

'Franziskaner'! Da hört sich doch alles auf! Er
Franziskaner There heard itself indeed everything on He
stops everything indeed

hat doch heute noch gar nichts getrunken?"
had indeed today still at all nothing drank

Das Herrle war links abgebogen und pfiff und
The little master was left curved off and whistled and
had turned left

schrie: "Bim! Mit mir gehst! Bim! Ja, weshalb
shouted Bim With me go (you) Bim Yes why

kommst du dann nicht?"
come you then not

Schließlich gab Bim als der Klügere nach und
Finally gave Bim as the smarter one after and
(in)

kam. Das hätte er nicht tun sollen, denn jetzt
came That had he not do should then now

legte ihn Pepi Bröselmeier an die Leine.
put him Pepi Broselmeyer on the leash

Das ging nicht so leicht, wie es gesagt ist. Es war
That went not so light as it said is It was
(easy)

eine recht schwierige Aufgabe für den
a truly difficult task for the

wohlbeleibten Herrn Pepi, sich bis zur Bimhöhe
well-embodied Mr Pepi himself until to the Bim-height
(large)

hinabzubeugen, und als er endlich unten angelangt
down to bow and as he finally under arrived

war, hatte sich Bim herumgedreht, und man kann
was had himself Bim turned around and one can

doch die Hundeleine nicht am Schwanz
indeed the dog-leash not at the tail

anknüpfen.
on-tie

Aber schließlich war Bim angekettet und lief, mit
But finally was Bim on-chained and walked with

sichtlichen Zeichen der Entrüstung,
visible signs of the indignation

neben seinem Herrn her. An jeder Straßenecke
next his master to At each street corner
next to his master

blieb er stehen und
remained he stand and

gab seiner Verachtung Ausdruck.
gave his despise expression
gave expression to his despise

Die Leute betrachteten schmunzelnd das Paar. Was
The people looked at chuckling the pair What
looked chuckling at the pair

wollte der Mann mit dem Spaten, der
wanted the man with the spade the

Soldatenmütze und dem Dackel? Aber Herr Pepi
soldier hat and the dachshund But Mr Pepi

achtete nicht auf die Gaffer. Was lag dran,
paid attention not on the gawper What lay there-on
What did it matter

was die Leute (sprich "Gschwerl") von ihm dachten,
what the people speak rabble from him thought

Leute, die wo nicht einmal eine Fülla (schreibe
people who well not once a villa write
(even)

"Villa") besaßen, viel weniger ein vierstöckiges
villa possessed much less a four floored

Mietshaus mit Zentralheizung und Lift in
tenant house with central heating and elevator in

Reparatur.
repair

"Wissen möchte ich, wo er hingeht?" dachte
Know may I where he goes to thought

sich Bim. "Jetzt is schon bald elfi und
(by) himself Bim Now (it) is already soon elevenish and

die Weißwurst im "Franziskaner" wird kalt!"
the white sausage in the Franziskaner becomes cold

Und bald erfuhr er das Ziel der Wanderung: die
And soon found out he the target of the walk the

Isaranlagen, allwo Bim seine erste
Isar (river) park where Bim his first

Unterrichtsstunde im Sanitätswesen erhalten
teaching hour in the sanitary business receive

sollte.
should

Ich muß jetzt leider einen Punkt berühren,
I must now unfortunately one point touch

dem ich bisher ängstlich aus dem Wege
which I until now fearfully out (of) the way

gegangen bin, um nicht in den Ruf eines
gone am for not in the call of an
(have)

erotischen Schriftstellers zu kommen: Bims
erotic *author* *to* *come* *Bim's*

Liebesleben in der Natur. Tja, das ist ein heikler
lovelive *in* *-the-* *nature* *Well* *that* *is* *a* *tricky*

Punkt. Bim verschwendete seine Gunstbezeigungen
point *Bim* *squandered* *his* *favors*

nicht nur an die Hündinnen der zwanzig Rassen,
not *just* *on* *the* *female dogs* *the* *twenty* *races*

von denen er abstammte, nein, dieser Wüstling
from *which* *he* *descended* *no* *this* *libertine*

wagte es, jedes Hundefräulein, das seine Bahn
dared *it* *each* *dog-miss* *that* *his* *track*

kreuzte, kurzweg anzusprechen und ihr in der
crossed *short-way* *to speak to* *and* *her* *in* *the*
(curtly)

Hundesprache verführerische Galanterien
dog language *seducing* *gallantry*

zuzuflüstern. "Fräulein Bernhardinerin sehen
to whisper to *Miss* *female St Bernard (dog)* *to look*
(looks)

heute wieder entzückend aus!" "Gnädigste Möpsin
today again delightful -out- gracious pug girl

werden mit jedem Wurf schlanker!" "Fräulein
becomes with each throw more slender Miss
(giving birth)

Windhund tragen ein todschickes Halsband! Wohl
greyhound to carry a dead-fancy collar Well
(carries) (very fashionable)

Familienerbstück?"
family inheritance piece
(family heirloom)

Auch angesichts dieser Künste konnte Herr Pepi
Also in face of this arts could Mr Pepi

mit Recht sagen: "Wo er das nur gerade her
with right say Who he that only now away
(truth)

hatte? Also von 'mir' hatte er es nicht!"
had Also from me had he it not

Sofort beim Eintritt in die Isarauen fiel
Already at the entry in the Isar area fell
{fiel auf; noticed}

nun dem Don Juan Bim eine braune Dackelin
now the Don Juan Bim a brown female dachshund

auf, eine   Dackelin   ... ich sage nur das eine
on   a   female dachshund   I   say   only   the   one

Wort "preisgekrönt".
word   prize crowned
       (award winning)

Aber die   "Dackelin"   wurde an der Leine
But   the   female dachshund   was   on   the   leash

geführt, Bim wurde an der Leine geführt - nur
led   Bim   was   on   the   leash   led   only

wer die Sehnsucht   kennt,   weiß, was sie
who the   desire   is familiar with   knows   what   they
                                             (how)

litten.
suffered

Es war ein heller, sonniger Herbsttag und immer
It   was   a   bright   sunny   autumn day   and   always

wieder frug Herr Pepi seinen Dackel: "Hörst, wie
again   asked   Mr   Pepi   his   dachshund   Hear   how

d' Amseln pfeif'n? Hörst du das?" und immer
th' blackbirds   whistle   Hear   you   that   and   always
(the)

wieder antwortete Bim in Gedanken: "Heute hatte
again answered Bim in thought Today had

es ihn derwischt! Ganz narret is er heute! Hatte
it him dervished Totally crazied is he today Had
    (made nuts)

er vielleicht 'denkt, das Amseln werden miauen?"
he maybe thought that blackbirds would mew

An einer Bank in den Anlagen, dicht am Ufer
On one bench in the park close to the (river)bank

der seichten Isar, band Herr Bröselmeier
of the shallow Isar (river) bound Mr Broselmeyer

seinen Hund fest, hielt ihm die Soldatenmütze
his dog fast held him the soldier hat

unter die Nase und schmeichelte:
under the nose and whispered

"Da, riech, Bim! Schön Witterung nehmen muß
There smell Bim Already scent take must

das Hunderl! Das Mützen suchen muß das
the little dog The hat search must the

gescheite Dackerl! Ja! Gelt, du bist
clever | little dachshund | Yes | Is valid {Right? (interjection)} | you | are

gescheit?"
clever

Bim warf einen scheelen Blick auf die Mütze.
Bim | threw | a | cross eyed | glance | on | the | hat

"Vollständig dari-dari is er heut!" dachte er.
Totally | crazy | is | he | today | thought | he

"Was geht mi das Mützen an!"
What | goes | me | the | hat | on
What do I care about that little hat

Und während Bim Betrachtungen darüber
And | while | Bim | observations | there-about

anstellte, daß jetzt die Weißwurst sicher längst
started | that | now | the | white sausage | surely | by far

gar geworden war, schaufelte der Herr
cooked | become | was | shoveled | -the- | Mr

Realitätenbesitzer schwitzend eine Grube. Wohl
real estate owner | sweating | a | pit | Well

zehnmal hielt er stöhnend in der Arbeit inne,
ten times held he groaning in the work pause

wischte sich den Schweiß von der Stirne und
wiped himself the sweat from the forehead and

brummte: "Und das soll gesund sein, hat der
grumbled And that should healthy be had the

Dokter gesagt! Aber jetzt wird sich's bald weis'n,
doctor said But now will itself it soon prove

ob die Dackeln Sanitäter sein oder nicht!"
whether the dachshunds sanitaries are or not
(sanitary dogs)

Endlich war die Grube brauchbar. Er legte die
Finally was the pit useful He put the

Mütze hinein und schaufelte locker Erde darüber.
hat to-in and shoveled loose earth there-over
(into it) (over it)

"Wird es schon finden, mein Bim! Fehlt sich
Will he already find my Bim Mistakes itself

nicht!"
not

Als er sich der Bank wieder zuwandte,
When he himself the (river) bank again towards turned

fand er dort einen freundlichen Herrn, der
found he there a friendly gentleman who

behaglich die Hände auf dem Rücken gefaltet
comfortably the hands on the back folded

hatte, und mit Bim scherzte.
had and with Bim joked

"Ein hübsches Mopserl haben Sie da!" meinte der
A pretty little pug have you there meant the
(said)

Herr.
gentleman

"Das is kein Mopserl!" fertigte ihn Pepi
That is not (a) little pug readied him Pepi
{abfertigen; deal with}

kurz ab. "Wann das ein Mopserl is, sind Sie
shortly off When that a little pug is are you

ein Rindviech!"
a beef creature
cattle

Mit   diesen   liebenswürdigen   Worten   band   er   den
With   these   amiable   words   bound   he   the

"guten   Hund"   los,   klatschte   in   die   Hände   und
good   dog   loose   clapped   in   the   hands   and

schrie: "Wo   ist   das   Mützerl?   Wo   ist?   Such,
shouted   Where   is   the   little hat   Where   is (it)   Search

Bim!"
Bim

Bim   schaute   ihn   groß   an.   Bei   dieser   Hitze   Mützen
Bim   looked   him   large   at   With   this   heat   hats
    Bim looked wide-eyed at him

suchen,   das   fehlte   ihm   grad   noch!
search   that   lacked   him   yet   still
                {gerade}

"Such,   Bim,   such!"
Search   Bim   search

Der   fremde   Herr   lachte,   und   der   Pepi
The   strange   gentleman   laughed   and   -the-   Pepi

Bröselmeier   ärgerte   sich.   "Du   kriegst   ein
Broselmeyer   irritated   himself   You   get   a
            got irritated   (will get)

Zuckerl,   Bim!   Ein   extragroßes   Zuckerl!
little sugar (cube)   Bim   An   extra large   little sugar cube

Wo   hat's   Herrle   s'   Mützerl   hingetan?"
Where   had it   little master   the   little hat   away-done
                    {das}   (put)

Der   Bim   wußte   ganz   genau,   wo   das   Herrle
The   Bim   knew   very   precise   where   the   little master

das   Mützerl   hingetan   hatte.   Er   hatte   ja   alles
that   little hat   away-done   had   He   had   indeed   all
                 (put)

mit   angesehen.   Aber   so   dumm   sein   wird   er   und
along   watched   But   so   dumb   be   would   he   and

sie   ausgraben!   Das   wär'   das   Neueste,   daß   er
it   dig out   That   would be   the   newest   that   he

gehorchen   tät!   Nein,   nein,   das   führte   der   Bim
obey   would do   No   no   that   carried   the   Bim
                                        (started)

nicht   ein.   Er   sprang   an   seinem   Herrn   empor,   lief
not   in   He   jumped   to   his   master   up   ran

in   die   Anlagen   und   fraß   Gras.
in   the   plantings   and   ate   grass

Der fremde Mann lachte aus Leibeskräften.
The strange man laughed out (of) life's forces
(all might)

"Das ist gar nicht zum Lachen!" schrie der Pepi
That is at all not to -the- laughing shouted -the- Pepi

und wurde jetzt ernstlich wild. "Was verstehen 'Sie'
and became now seriously wild What understand you

vom Hundsdressieren! Gehen Sie heim und
from the dog training Go you home and

belästigen S' die Leute nicht, Sie Hammel, Sie
bother you the people not you mutton you
{Sie}

ganz ausgeschamter! Und du, Bim, Hundsviech,
totally shameless one And you Bim dog creature

miserabliches, hörst jetz gleich auf mit
miserable hear now immediately up with
{aufhören; stop}

der Spinatfresserei!! Suchst jetz gleich das
the spinach guzzling Search now immediately the

Mützerl, Bankert, elendiger! Da gehst her oder
little hat rascal miserable one There go away or

i hau dir das Mordstrumm Spaten um deine
I chop you the murder piece spade around your
(great piece of)

scheinheiligen Ohrwascheln! Herrgottsakrament
hypocritical earflaps Lord-god-sacrament

übereinander, willst jetzt parieren oder nicht?!"
over-one-another will (you) now obey or not

Der Bim wollte nicht.
The Bim wanted not

Wie er das Herrle so schimpfen hörte, sagte
As he the little master like that scold heard said

er sich: "Jetzt ist die Tollwut bei ihm
he himself Now is the rabies at him

ausgebrochen!" setzte sich in Galopp und lief in
broken out set himself in trot and ran into

die Isar.
the Isar (river)

Und was sah sein beglücktes Auge da?
And what saw his delighted eye there

Susanna   im   Bade!
Susanna   in the   bath

Da   schwamm sie, die herrliche   Dackelin,   und
There   swam   she the   lovely   female dachshund and

warf ihm einen Blick zu - einen Blick...!! "Ewig
threw him   a   glance at   a   glance   eternally

dein!"
yours

Und   sie   schwammen   um die Wette,   isarabwärts,
And   they   swam   for the bet   down the Isar
   a race

nach der Eisenbahnbrücke   zu - und in den
to   the   iron-track-bridge   -to-   and in the
   (railbridge)

Isaranlagen   stand ein Mann und brüllte: "Bim!
Isar-park   stood a man and roared   Bim

Biiiiiim!" Und   immer aufgeregter und beinahe
Biiiiiim   And   always more excited and almost

weinerlich: "Bim! I tue dir ja nichts!" und zuletzt
whiny   Bim I do you well nothing and at last
   I won't hurt you

ganz verzweifelnd: "Bim - gutes Hunderl - komm
all   despairing   Bim   good   little dog   come

doch bloß, ich gib dir das   Zuckerl!   Wenn du
indeed   just   I   give you the   little sugar (cube) When   you

nur gerade kommst!!"
only   directly   come

Aber nicht der Bim kam, sondern der fremde
But   not   the   Bim   came   but   the   weird

Herr   trat näher, nahm die Hände vom
gentleman stepped closer   took   the   hands   from the

Rücken, in denen jetzt die grüne Mütze sichtbar
back   in   which   now   the   green   hat   visible

ward, die ihn als Anlagenaufseher legitimierte, und
became that him   as   park-overseer   legitimated   and

sprach gewichtig: "Nämlich, wie heißen Sie dann
spoke   weighty   Namely   how   are called you   then
           (importantly)

nachher?"
after-to

"Das ist a Gemeinheit!" schrie der Pepi. "Das ist
That is a meanness shouted the Pepi That is

eine ganz hinterlistige Zweispältigkeit ist das!"
a totally deceitful duality is that

"Nehme Sie Ihnen in Obacht!" drohte das
Take you yourself in guard threatened the

städtische Amtsorgan. "Sonst mach i Ihnen
city functionary Otherwise make I you
{Ich}

zuwegen Amtsbeleidingung kriminalisch, mein
because of insult of office criminally my

Lieber!"
love

"Und derweil versauft der Bim!" jammerte Pepi
And meanwhile drowns -the- Bim wailed Pepi

Bröselmeier und wollte davonlaufen. Aber der
Broselmeyer and wanted to run there from But the

Aufseher hielt ihn am Ärmel fest und donnerte:
overseer held him by the arms fast and thundered

"Da bleiben Sie!! Im Namen des Gesätzes!"
There stay you In the name of the law

Und weil der Pepi nicht mit dem Namen des
And because -the- Pepi not with the name of the

Gesätzes zu tun haben wollte, blieb er halt da.
law to do have wanted stayed he just there

Und sein Name wurde aufgeschrieben und sein
And his name was written down and his

Stand und die Wohnung und sein halber
position and the house and his half

Stammbaum dazu, weil wir ordnungsliebende
family tree there-to since we order-loving
(as well)

Behörden haben.
authorities have

Noch eine geschlagene halbe Stunde ist der Pepi
Still one struck half hour is -the- Pepi

nachher in den Isaranlagen umhergeirrt und hat
after that in the Isar park wander around and had

den Bim gesucht und sich einen riesigen Durst
-the- Bim sought and himself a giant thirst

angeschrieen.
shouted onto

Und hätt' sich doch diese Mühe sparen können!
And had himself indeed this trouble spare be able

Denn wie er zerschmettert, den Spaten unter'm
Then as he crushed the late one under the

Arm, im "Bürgerbräu" ankam, da empfing ihn die
arm in the Citizen-brew arrived then received him the

Kellnerin mit den Worten: "Gerade ist Ihr
waitress with the words Now has your

Foxl gekommen!"
little Fox(hound) arrived

Richtig, da saß er unter dem Stammtisch, nagte
Truly there sat he under the regular table gnawed

an einem Knochen und zwinkerte seinem Herrle
on a bone and winked his little master

161

einen Blick zu, der ungefähr besagte:
a glance at that approximately said

"Bist jetzt wieder so weit, daß mann mit dir
Are you again so far that one with you

verkehren könnte?"
associate can

Und drei Minuten später saß Bim auf Herrles
And three minutes later saw Bim on little master's

Schoß und hörte herablassend dessen Bitte um
lap and heard condescending that one's plea for

Verzeihung an: "Brauchst kein Sanitätsdackel
forgiveness to (You) need no sanitary dachshund

werden, Bim! Naa, naa, das überlassen mal das
become Bim No no that (we) leave over just the

spinneten Schäferhund'! Weil's du nur gerade
crazy shepherd -dog- Because it you just now

wieder da bist!"
again there are

Und   zwei   Tage   später   war   auch   ein   polizeilicher
And   two   days   later   was   also   a   policy

Strafbefehl   "gerade   wieder   da".   Wegen
punitive order   now   again   there   Because

"vorschriftswidriger   Verwüstung   der   städtischen
regulation-adverse   destruction   of the   city

Isaranlagen   und   wiederholtem   Freilaufenlassen   eines
Isar plantings   and   repeated   free-walk-let   of a
(unleashed walking)

Zwergpudels".
dwarf poodle

www.ingramcontent.com/pod-product-compliance
Lightning Source LLC
LaVergne TN
LVHW011330080426
835513LV00006B/263